THE
BRIDGE
TO
GROWTH

THE
BRIDGE
TO
GROWTH

**HOW SERVANT LEADERS ACHIEVE BETTER RESULTS
AND WHY IT MATTERS NOW MORE THAN EVER**

JUDE RAKE

Skyhorse Publishing

Skyhorse Publishing books may be purchased in bulk at special discounts for sales promotion, corporate gifts, fund-raising, or educational purposes. Special editions can also be created to specifications. For details, contact the Special Sales Department, Skyhorse Publishing, 307 West 36th Street, 11th Floor, New York, NY 10018 or info@skyhorsepublishing.com.

Skyhorse® and Skyhorse Publishing® are registered trademarks of Skyhorse Publishing, Inc.®, a Delaware corporation.

Visit our website at www.skyhorsepublishing.com.

10 9 8 7 6 5 4 3 2 1

Library of Congress Cataloging-in-Publication Data is available on file.

Cover design by Rain Saukas

Print ISBN: 978-1-5107-2840-0
Ebook ISBN: 978-1-5107-2841-7

Printed in the United States of America

To Kathy

I dedicate this book to my beautiful wife for fueling my growth in so many ways. Your guidance regarding the principles detailed in this book, your unwavering support, and your love have made this life an incredible joy ride.

Table of Contents

Preface

The goal of *The Bridge to Growth* is to help leaders and emerging leaders achieve personal, professional, and financial growth. It's the same goal upon which I founded my firm, JDR Growth Partners.

This is intentionally a short book, and I've attempted to maximize useful-insight-per-page. I sought the advice of several authors and pundits. A few of them—perhaps well meaning—suggested that I add superfluous content that would help me sell more books. I eventually realized that it was exactly this approach that had fueled the creation of the many business books I never finished (even though I started them with enthusiasm). I frequently found most of the value in the first half of the book, and the remainder skimmable at best. I did not want to create that kind of book.

To maximize useful insight from cover to cover, I used a framework akin to an executive memo. For those who prefer processing information with some degree of linearity, this will probably connect with you. Chapters are structured around nine guiding principles. Each chapter includes a short introduction, a statement of The Leadership Principle, a set-up of the problem titled The Leader's Challenge, my assessment of What Matters Most, and at least one Success Model to help bring the principle to life based on my experiences. I also promise useful tips and tools throughout, but no fluff.

There's an age-old debate in the business world: What's more important, strategy or execution? I believe both are critical. But what if something else is just as important? What if there is a third ingredient to business success, one that many companies undervalue, namely servant leadership?

Informed by my 35-plus years of leading high performance teams and over a decade as a president and CEO, *The Bridge to Growth* reveals how servant leaders bridge strategy into exceptional execution by elevating the commitment and performance of the people they lead.

In today's business climate, the cadence between strategy and execution is compressing, making the integration of the two more important than ever. Too many workers are being left out of this equation. More and more people are disconnected from their company's goals, even though they still report being satisfied with their jobs. A Global Workforce Survey conducted by Towers Watson revealed that a mere 21 percent of workers feel engaged and truly committed to their company's success and goals, even though 86 percent report liking their jobs. Is this reflective of a failure of leadership, a shift in the attitudes of today's workers, or both?

Apparently, many people are settling for a job that satisfies their basic needs, yet denies them a motivating answer to two important questions: "How does my personal work connect to my company's goals, and how can I help us achieve them?" In these cases, leaders have unfortunately failed to fully engage workers in either the development or execution of their company's mission, goals, and ultimately its journey toward success or failure. Too often, workers are being over-managed and under-led. I believe this "commitment gap" represents the largest source of untapped potential to create economic value in our society today.

How can leaders tap into this gap and raise the performance bar? This question matters more now than it ever has. As our world becomes more socially connected, more women progress into leadership roles, and millennials seek more meaning and purpose in their work than previous generations did, the principles of servant leadership are becoming more relevant than ever before.

I believe leadership is both art and science, and that it can be learned. For almost four decades, I've been a voracious student of leadership, and I've been fortunate to work with some outstanding leaders. In this book, I've captured much of what I've learned. *The Bridge to Growth* provides leaders, emerging leaders, stakeholders, and board members a blueprint of nine proven leadership principles to move the people you lead from satisfactorily disengaged to enthusiastically committed to making a difference and winning.

If you are interested in growing as a leader—and if you perhaps also agree that many aspects of great leadership are *not* innate—you have my promise that this book is worth your time.

Introduction

Most leaders ascend to ever-increasing levels of influence because they are smart and assertive, and because they deliver good results—and *not* necessarily because they are great at bringing out the best in other people. Yet leading people becomes increasingly important the higher one ascends. Could this be why so many would-be leaders struggle once they reach senior leadership positions in businesses, schools, governments, churches, and other organizations?

Unfortunately, many organizations treat leadership as though it is an innate ability. Something you're born with. Something that just happens naturally. While organizations readily invest in teaching their employees routine or requisite skills, they provide little development when it comes to leading people. This is one reason why so many organizations are under-led and over-managed, and why so many people feel disengaged from their organization's mission and goals.

Almost every leader fights the creeping feeling that his or her team could be achieving more. These leaders constantly wonder if they are doing everything possible to enable the success of the people they lead. I believe the best leaders feel these yearnings the most. While they are beholden to the stakeholders who hired them, these leaders are also driven by the sense of responsibility they feel toward their workforce.

My most significant personal confrontation with this dilemma happened early in my career when I was promoted to Business Vice President at SC Johnson, replacing Fisk Johnson as he moved upstairs to eventually take the company leadership reigns from his father, Sam Johnson, upon his retirement. It was a big step in my career. I transitioned from an emerging leader role—heading a small, albeit very successful team—into a corporate officer role leading one of the company's largest divisions. Our CEO at the time was fond of working with The Boston Consulting Group (BCG), with whom I would now be paired. They were tasked with analyzing our current situation and recommending a strategy for accelerating profitable growth of the division I now led. As I built and launched my leadership team, and BCG performed their analytics in parallel, I became increasingly concerned about the separation between the two. While the BCG consultants were clearly very bright, they lacked experience and were not digging into the business as much as I had expected them to. I sensed that the project was streaming toward strategic recommendations that might be too superficial in nature, and not adequately grounded in facts and research. Worse, my leadership team increasingly did not want to be bothered by the consulting project at all! They viewed the consultants as a distraction from the day-to-day reality and demands of their roles and responsibilities. They had real and pressing work to do. I began to worry that BCG would develop a plan for which none of my team felt ownership. I knew such a plan would be doomed to fail.

Instead of offloading this important work, I sat down with our BCG teammates and with my leadership team, and led them in the development of a more collaborative strategic planning process (that is defined in more detail in Chapter 3, so I will not belabor it here). Because we invested the time and energy to engage our workforce more intentionally in the planning process, we achieved increased workforce collaboration and commitment to the plan we ultimately developed and executed. It led to unprecedented profitable growth of SCJ's home cleaning division over the next four years and a strategic planning process that I would go on to use for many years to force-multiply my leadership influence, elevate workforce engagement, and significantly improve the financial performance of several businesses.

THE LEADER'S CHALLENGE

Most leaders are inundated with multiple urgent responsibilities that demand their attention and can distract them from things that matter most. It's easy for leaders to dedicate most of their time and energy to managing the countless fires that always seem to be threatening their organizations. The remainder of their time can be consumed by the need to develop productive relationships with the stakeholders that control resources they need to survive and prosper. Strategy, talent development, nurturing a healthy culture, and building workforce commitment can feel like luxuries appropriate to address only when time permits. Unfortunately, time rarely does permit, and leaders who travel down this well-worn path deliver sub-optimal results while wondering why their workforce doesn't perform at a higher level.

I saw this happen very early in my career, shortly after graduate school, as a young brand manager at The Clorox Company. The Federal Trade Commission had forced Procter & Gamble (P&G) to divest of Clorox in 1969 for anti-trust reasons. Clorox went on to have a very impressive run creating, buying, and expanding many brands, from Formula 409 to Kingsford Charcoal. By the time I joined the company in 1986, most of the senior leaders had been trained at P&G, one of the best business training and leadership development grounds in the world, in my opinion. Clorox had also become widely known for excellent training and development of marketers and general managers, and there were many strong leaders between me and the senior leaders of the company (including Doug Kellam, Glenn Savage, Bill Morissey, and Craig Sullivan).

Clorox was led by a CEO and a president who were intent upon taking Clorox into the detergent category to compete against P&G. It was the biggest project in the entire company, and those who proved their mettle were often assigned to the team. After two successful years on other brands, I was assigned to work on this initiative and quickly gained an illuminating view of different leadership styles—styles that would inform my own for the rest of my career.

At the time, the large German company Henkel AG owned roughly 30 percent of Clorox, so the CEO and president reported to them regularly. Despite the best efforts of a very talented team working on the detergent project, it was becoming increasingly clear that this initiative was the wrong direction for the company, both strategically and financially. I watched as senior management slightly modified reports of my talented management team for presentation to Henkel and our board of directors. To be clear, they weren't exactly falsified, but the final product told what I call "partial truths." While I was impressed with my immediate managers, we rarely saw the CEO or the president; they remained on another floor of the company in executive suites that required special clearance for entry. The only time I saw them was the rare visit to their office to prep them for a meeting with Henkel or the board of directors.

I was eventually recruited away from Clorox by a former colleague, Scott Langmack, who had left Clorox to lead marketing and business development at Pepsi Cola International. I was excited to broaden my skill base and grow as a leader. I had never even travelled outside of the borders of the United States, and I was about to embark on a role that would transport me to twenty-eight countries over the next few years. I didn't take this new role because I did not like working at Clorox. In fact, I thoroughly enjoyed the people and the culture we had on our team (and across the household products division). In the moment, it was a tough decision to leave. But over time, I started looking upon the senior leadership of Clorox with skepticism, and I vowed to never corridor myself off from the workforce like they had if I ever ascended into a senior leadership role. Not surprisingly, the detergent project was eventually shelved much later than it should have been—after costing the company millions in losses—and the CEO and the president both retired early. It remains one of the few large blemishes in Clorox's forty-eight-year history.

WHAT MATTERS MOST

I noted earlier that the cadence between strategy and execution is compressing, making the integration of the two more important than ever. But too many workers are being left out of this equation. We hear it all the time—leaders must motivate and fully engage the people they lead. But how? Increasingly, they can't just assume that everyone will follow them just because they are the boss. That sounds fairly obvious, but mounting evidence suggests a gap between this leadership style and reality. A recent workforce survey by Franklin Covey revealed:

- Only 15 percent of workforce respondents could name even one of the top three goals their leaders had identified.
- Among those who *could* name a goal, only 51 percent said they were committed to achieving it.
- 81 percent of everyone surveyed said they were not held accountable to progress against the company's goals.
- 87 percent said they had no idea what to do to help the company achieve the goals.

Equally startling, a global survey of over 90,000 workers by Towers Watson uncovered:

- Only 21 percent of employees are truly engaged in their work, saying they would "go the extra mile."
- 38 percent are mostly or entirely disengaged.
- Only 38 percent believe that senior management is sincerely interested in their well-being.
- Less than 40 percent believe senior management communicates openly and honestly.
- Just 44 percent believe that senior management tries to be visible and accessible.
- Less than half believe that senior management actions are consistent with the company's core values.
- Yet 86 percent like or love their jobs!

In *The Three Signs of a Miserable Job*, Patrick Lincioni suggests that people disengage for the following reasons:

- **Anonymity:** they feel their leaders don't know or care what they are doing.

- **Irrelevance:** they don't understand how their job makes a difference.
- **Immeasurability:** they cannot measure or assess for themselves the contribution they are making.

This is an indictment of traditional leadership, and it is why I believe that many companies are over-managed and under-led. What if 100 percent of the people in a company said they were "all in?" What impact would going from 21 percent engagement to 100 percent engagement have on results? According to a recent Gallup survey, engaged employees are 21 percent more productive, have 37 percent less absenteeism, and have 25 percent lower turnover. A study by Vance found that companies with highly engaged employees score between 12 and 34 percent higher in customer satisfaction ratings. And my favorite study by Aon Hewitt found that companies in the top quartile of employee engagement scores generated 50 percent higher total shareholder return than the average company. You do the math. Of all the levers a leader has at her fingertips to improve results, this is the biggest and most often under-leveraged.

SERVANT LEADERSHIP

Back in the early 1990's, I read Max DePree's book titled *Leadership is an Art*. I found his insights regarding servant leadership inspiring because he articulated the leader's responsibilities to the people he leads in more personal, human, and engaging language than I had read or heard before. And to give credit where credit is due, Robert K. Greanleaf first introduced the servant leader concept in 1970 when he published his essay entitled "The Servant as Leader." That essay was later expanded into a book, and the servant leadership movement was born.

I was first exposed to the servant leader concept at a time when my career was blossoming and I was rising up the corporate ladder, yet I was not feeling inspired by most of the leaders I studied above my immediate supervisor. In fact, I was having serious doubts about the desirability of ascending into the senior management ranks. Other than their paychecks, there wasn't much about the existing models that I found appealing, and I had serious reservations about how well I would fit into the executive suite. I had grown up in rural, blue collar Indiana and I found most of the senior leaders I was encountering woefully out of touch with the people on the front lines of the business. I was convinced that future leaders needed to be more empathic and in touch with the people they aspired to lead, and Max DePree gave me hope that this was possible.

The best servant leaders are not "soft" as some might think. They have a very high performance bar. But they balance high expectations with caring leadership that inspires the people they lead to raise the bar even higher and achieve extraordinary results.

Since then I've had the good fortune to meet with—and in some cases work with—experts on this topic such as Steven Covey, Jack Welch, Jim Collins, Tom Peters, and Patrick Lincioni. I don't need to tell you that their lessons on leadership are legendary. They teach us that the best leaders are typically not the ones we read and hear about in the media. In *Good to Great*, Jim Collins refers to these as Level 5 leaders. In Max DePree's assessment, these leaders typically take more than their fair share of the blame for stumbles and give credit to those they lead for successes. They also realize that they need all hands on deck to achieve the full potential of their

company. Servant leaders are force-multipliers, not just force directors. They bring out the best in the people they lead, and they don't
settle for a mere 21 percent of their workforce being willing to step
up and go the extra mile. They serve rather than merely command
the people in their company by giving employees what they need to
fully engage and commit to achieving the company's goals.

**Servant leaders focus relentlessly on moving more
of their workforce beyond being satisfactorily
disengaged toward eagerly committed to making
a difference.**

Many people go through life never experiencing a compelling leader like this, which is why I feel privileged to have
worked with several of them. I also had the good fortune of
learning from a few exceptional sports coaches earlier in my life
who helped me understand what it takes to win. My football
coaches, Bill Mumford and Joe Cequeira, taught me that hustle
often trumps talent when talent doesn't give it everything it has.
Because of their examples and leadership, I learned early to rel-
ish the role of the underdog. Later in life, as a basketball coach
myself, I was fortunate to experience the leadership influence of
Pat Summitt. Pat was a model for balancing the forces of competitive intensity, empowerment, and caring with an incredible
desire to win. (More about Pat later in Chapter 1.)

None of these leaders and coaches was perfect, but each taught
me something special that I was able to blend into my blueprint
of leadership principles that I follow. Over the past three-plus
decades, I leveraged these nine proven principles while leading
high performance teams building world-class brands, profitably

growing big and small businesses, and increasing the economic value of publicly-held, family owned, and private equity backed companies across a variety of industries. I also used them to elevate workforce engagement, collaboration, innovation, and accountability to bridge strategy into exceptional execution and results.

The Nine Proven Leadership Principles

1. Grow leaders and difference-makers, not just followers.
2. Build and orchestrate synergistic, high performance teams more powerful than the sum of their parts.
3. Focus your organization on strategic priorities and simplify operations to accelerate progress.
4. Champion the people who purchase and use your products and services.
5. Cultivate a performance-based culture of innovation that unleashes the innate desire in the people you lead to solve, create, and contribute to winning.
6. Communicate relentlessly to give your workforce the context they need to sign up for and truly commit to achieving company goals.
7. See the world through the eyes of others, and your example will breed a healthier organization.
8. Be the model you want emulated. Operate transparently, deliver on your promises, and remain steadfastly focused on doing the right things.
9. Coach people to achieve more than they thought possible. They need a model of success more than they need a critic. Inspire your entire organization to step up by revealing what success looks like, catching people doing something well, and showing your gratitude publicly.

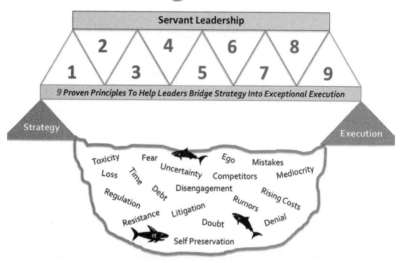

It's been many years since I first read Max DePree's book about servant leadership. Yet I've come to believe that servant leadership will ultimately be the only kind of leadership still standing. Sure, it's not for everyone, because it's harder in the short term than simply implementing autocratic or laissez-faire models. But assuming a potential leader has the requisite skills to do the job, I believe my proven leadership principles can help catapult her toward successfully achieving the success and growth she desires.

In Chapter 1, we'll begin the journey across the bridge by diving into the first principle. Together we'll explore a challenge all leaders face, learn what matters most, and review a success model. And throughout the book you'll get a chance to meet some of the leaders, coaches, and mentors that informed and helped me develop the nine principles. Onward!

Part One

The Foundation

Chapter 1

The Most Important Thing Leaders Do

L eadership is an exponential equation. That means the best leaders have a force-multiplying impact on their entire organization. They cultivate other great leaders who develop difference-makers into even more great leaders. This proliferation of leadership throughout the organization drives improved performance, which is the true exponential effect of a force-multiplying leader.

LEADERSHIP PRINCIPLE #1

Servant leaders grow leaders and difference-makers, not just followers.

THE LEADER'S CHALLENGE

Developing the talents and capabilities of the people in an organization takes time, energy, and empathy. Empathy is a so-called "soft skill" some people view as unnecessary in the rough and tumble world of business. They'll ask: "Why should empathy matter when being a hard-charger is what gets you promoted?" Most companies and senior managers channel their priceless time and energy toward urgent issues and business-building projects to show how action-oriented they are, not on developing the talents of their people. Furthermore, when times get tough, many companies relegate talent and leadership development to the HR department, believing that leaders ought to focus on more pressing and important initiatives. They treat this as a luxury rather than the necessity it is.

WHAT MATTERS MOST

The most important thing leaders do is deliver results that meet or exceed goals. The best leaders know that they must have leaders at all levels of their company to make this happen.

When it comes to driving the results they desire, the best leaders sincerely believe that nothing is more important than talent and leadership development. They pay more than lip service to it. They do everything possible to cultivate a high-performing team that cascades this conviction and approach throughout their organization to maximize leadership at all levels—and this includes building empathy (which I discuss later in Chapter 7). They do not *delegate* it to HR! They *partner* with HR to make it happen! The best leaders teach their team and their entire organization to drive differentiation of talent, and they reward difference-makers. They understand that feeding the talent development equation illustrated below is the best way to fuel improved results and sustained growth.

Skills   Attitude   Coaching   Results   Potential

Organizations inherently regress toward the mean when supervisors avoid candid discussions regarding performance. This problem is compounded when rewards are allocated homogeneously to appease the masses. The best leaders realize that grade inflation only leads to mediocrity. They also believe with passion that all people deserve an honest assessment of performance and career prospects because life is too short for anyone to hang out in a dead-end job without honest feedback. The best leaders understand that poor performers repel difference-makers, block the advancement of talented players, and call into question the judgment of the leaders who tolerate poor performance. Servant leaders don't avoid the brutal facts in the interest of empathy. Instead, they have the courage and integrity to embrace tough discussions with poor performers and give them every chance to improve. If coaching with empathy and candor fails to yield improved results, they guide poor performers out of their organization with compassion, dignity, and support.

Servant leaders resist the inertial pull of the organization to homogenize by continually differentiating talent and performance.

I struggled with this concept early in my career because I felt overly responsible for the people I led. I wanted to save everyone. As a relatively new supervisor, if someone above me suggested we might need to terminate one of my supervisees due to poor performance, I became even more determined to "fix" them. This instinct served me well because I was able to coach and develop quite a few people to improved performance and a successful career, but over time I learned that some people are not savable, and the effort to save them comes with significant opportunity cost. Everyone deserves good coaching and a chance to improve, to a point. But they also deserve an honest assessment when the fit between the challenges of the job at hand and their capabilities and their potential is not a good match.

The first time I had to fire an employee was incredibly difficult for me. The process doesn't bother some supervisors so much, but I found it very challenging. Even with time and experience, I still find it difficult. However, staying in touch with some people I have outplaced and seeing them matriculate to positions in which they are much happier because they've found a job that is a better fit for them has helped me enormously.

When it comes to talent development, it's easy to become overly distracted by poorer performers. But the best leaders know that the bulk of their coaching energy must be spent on personally championing difference-makers who maximize the equation above. Otherwise they will lose them to an organization that does. Effective leaders don't relegate talent management and development to HR because they realize that it is the leader personally who must be the Chief Talent Officer (even if they do have outstanding HR teammates). In Chapter 9, I'll provide specific examples of how servant leaders can coach difference-makers to achieve more than they ever thought possible.

You might think I'm being idealistic or optimistic, given how much engaged business leaders have on their plates. And it's true! They must help the team articulate a compelling vision, purpose, and strategic direction for the organization. They must work collaboratively to define and champion the organization's core values to which people genuinely commit. They must relentlessly walk the talk because everyone is watching every move they make. They must communicate transparently and provide the context the workforce needs to step up to the challenges they face and achieve peak performance. Most importantly, they *must* deliver results that meet or exceed the expectations of their stakeholders. It's a tall order. No question.

But even if a leader accomplishes all of this with excellence, he will still likely fail over the long haul if he expects his workforce to simply follow him to the promised land just because he is the boss. No matter how charismatic and motivating a leader might be, execution and results will not be exceptional *and* sustainable without leadership at all levels of the organization. If everyone is merely following and "managing up," then the leader becomes a bottleneck and the company will be forever throttled by the leader's personal capacity.

A SUCCESS MODEL

Several years ago when I was COO at a large consumer products company, we needed a keynote speaker for our annual marketing and sales meeting. Given that our company was a big sponsor of NCAA women's college basketball, we decided to invite Pat Summitt to be our keynote speaker. Pat was the legendary coach at The University of Tennessee for thirty-eight years. She still holds the record for the most all-time wins for a coach in NCAA basketball history for men or women in any division.

Pat inspired everyone with her energy and her famous "Definite Dozen Leadership Traits for On and Off the Court Success." After our meeting at dinner, I shared with Pat that I had coached youth basketball for many years. She graciously took interest, and invited me to be a guest coach at a Lady Vols game. I was floored! I took her up on her offer and eventually travelled to Knoxville for an unforgettable weekend.

I knew that Pat was an outstanding coach, and I admired her for her accomplishments, but I had no idea just how good she was at cultivating leaders throughout the Lady Vols basketball program. From the moment I stepped onto that campus, everything was executed with excellence. I soon learned that I would be shadowing Pat with the parents of a few prospective recruits, including Candace Parker (the top-rated high school player and eventual national Player of the Year at Tennessee). I discovered firsthand why so many recruits chose the Lady Vols program, and why so many former players and coaches use terms of endearment when recalling Pat Summitt's influence on their lives.

Game day was quite a production, from pre-game activities to post-game reception. Anyone who watched Pat from the sidelines might expect her to lead everything with an iron fist. It was quite the opposite. Pat was clearly orchestrating everything . . . but the entire weekend *appeared* to be executed by everyone *but* Pat. She had done most of her leading and coaching *in practice*. The assistant coaches and players stepped up to the plate time and again, as did her administrative support staff. They took turns leading, and they collaboratively leaned on each other's strengths to elevate performance throughout game day activities.

During the game, we sat immediately behind Pat and the team. At halftime the Lady Vols were trailing. We went into the locker room with the team. Pat was not there. I watched as the players—by themselves—took turns facilitating a brainstorming session about what had worked well and what needed improvement. Then they presented their analysis to the assistant coaches for input and guidance. Clearly, these players and assistant coaches had been trained well. They knew what to do without being micro-managed. Finally, Pat joined the team, and the players and assistant coaches collectively presented their conclusions. Pat succinctly graded their performance and assessments, added her own personal evaluations, and they aligned on an action plan for the second half. Everyone had led at some point. They leaned on each other's strengths and focused on the biggest opportunities for improvement. They debated vigorously and respectfully. Ownership was achieved. There was no lecture or screaming. Halftime ended with a quintessential Pat Summitt inspirational call to heightened intensity and hustle, and the team went out and kicked their opponents' behinds!

For me, this was an impressive example of a leader growing leaders and difference-makers, not just demanding followership. Is it any wonder that Pat had one of the highest graduation rates of any coach in history? Is it any wonder that so many former Lady Vols have gone on to become leaders in so many walks of life? Michelle Brooke-Marciniak, who became coach at the University of South Carolina Gamecocks as well as a successful business leader and ESPN's Kara Lawson, one of the best college and NBA basketball analysts, are but a few examples. Pat Summitt showed us that leaders can be demanding, passionate, and ultra-competitive, yet still focus a significant amount of their time, energy, and empathy on the development of leaders at all levels of their organization. It's what fueled her unprecedented results at Tennessee, and it's the most important thing leaders do.

Chapter 2

Individuals Play the Game, but Teams Beat the Odds

In America, we treasure independence and freedom. It's in our DNA. It's easy to understand why if you've read *1776* by David McCollough, an outstanding book that gave me a deeper appreciation of the principle-based sacrifices our founders made to achieve the freedom many take for granted.

I would never suggest that our cultural disposition toward independence is a bad thing. But like most strengths, it can sometimes get in the way of our goals—especially when we want to accomplish something that is bigger than what we can hope to achieve individually.

LEADERSHIP PRINCIPLE #2

Servant leaders build and orchestrate synergistic, high performance teams that are more powerful than the sum of their parts.

THE LEADER'S CHALLENGE

Leading is getting harder and harder in every walk of life.

Stakeholders demand improved performance and bottom line results faster than ever before. Leadership tenure is shrinking everywhere you look, from CEOs to head coaches to leaders of non-profit organizations, and even at some academic institutions. The pressure for performance continues to rise.

In response, some leaders try to pull the "easy lever" by surrounding themselves with people who agree with their every decision and who always do what they are told. The temptation to fall into this trap is great given the increasing need for fast results, even when the leader knows better. In the heat of battle, while tackling urgent challenges and opportunities, execution is likely to be faster when direct reports fall in line with the wishes of the leader. In the short term, this is always going to be true. However, this can also become a trap which saps an organization of vibrant energy, innovation, commitment, and, ultimately, ownership of results over the longer term. If everyone is merely following and managing up, the leader's bandwidth limits the entire organization's ability to grow.

On the flip side, another tempting "easy lever" is to follow the guidance offered by one of the most "liked" calls to action on LinkedIn: "Hire great people and get out of their way." I think many of the people who "like" this statement are just tired of being micro-managed. However, this is ultimately a dangerous leadership principle because it can translate to an abdication of responsibility. Leadership is a contact sport. Can you imagine a quarterback simply stepping back and saying, "You guys are great, now go get 'em! I'll be over here"? Leaders should not be in the way, but they'd better be in the game, arm-in-arm and leading their team.

WHAT MATTERS MOST

Individuals play the game, but teams beat the odds. Full disclosure: I borrowed that saying from the US Navy Seals, an organization I respect and admire. The best leaders surround themselves with the most talented people they can possibly find, and they are secure enough to hire people who are better than they are in key areas of responsibility. Most importantly, they build high-performing cross-functional teams with complementary skills that augment and fuel each others' strengths and offset or at least mitigate weaknesses.

Building a high performance team is as much art as it is science. The best leaders think like engineers and "feel" like artists. Teams are a lot like living, breathing organisms that respond to many variables that leaders must persistently tinker with and balance. These variables should be attended to as vigorously as a master gardener who weeds, fertilizes, waters, and prunes a garden. The old days of promoting people onto teams based entirely on relationships or individual results are over. Of course, results matter . . . but *how* results are achieved matters more than ever, because we know that tapping into individual behavioral preferences and core values to create team synergy can make all the difference.

Servant leaders pay special attention to team chemistry and behavioral preferences.

Consider the performance of the San Antonio Spurs. The Spurs have been the champions of the National Basketball Association five times over the past two decades. If you stack up the individual achievements and talents of the members of each of their championship teams against those of their opponents, the awards and credentials of all five of their championship teams pale in comparison. But the Spurs have still won because they have played better *as a team,* leveraging complementary skills and synergies to beat their more "talented" and "athletic" opponents. The 2014 NBA Finals against the Miami Heat was a classic example. Many people considered the 2014 Miami Heat to be the most talented NBA team ever assembled at the time. The Spurs didn't just beat them—they destroyed them.

Next we'll dive into how to build a high performance team, but first I want to define what success looks like from my perspective. Below you'll find the ten most important traits of high performance teams that I've identified over the years based on both sport and business experience, on outstanding team training and development at The Center For Creative Leadership, The Booth School of Business at The University of Chicago, The Kellogg School of Management at Northwestern University, and on extensive reading about the US military special forces and The Navy Seals. The best teams I've served on, built, or led exhibited these ten traits.

The Ten Most Important Traits of High Performance Teams

1. **Synergy:** Team members complement each other's strengths, weaknesses, and behavioral preferences.
2. **Commitment:** Team members are fully committed to the team's success, and they are willing to sacrifice their egos for the good of the team.
3. **Constructive Contention:** The toughest challenges and issues are put on the table and debated vigorously. Team members are passionate and unguarded, and everyone commits to and supports resolutions and next steps, even when consensus is not possible.
4. **Accountability:** Even though there is usually a designated leader, team leadership is often shared. Team members hold each other accountable, challenge and help each other, and are deeply concerned about letting down their teammates.

5. **Purpose:** The team develops shared goals, purpose, and core values aligned with stakeholder needs.

6. **Rewards:** The team shares in significant rewards for achieving their goals and even bigger rewards for exceeding expectations.

7. **Transparency:** Communication is fluid and transparent, and all information is shared openly and candidly. New digital tools make this much easier today than yesterday.

8. **Collaboration:** Team members exude a "we are stronger than me" attitude by breaking down silos, working across functional boundaries, and proactively tapping into each other's strengths.

9. **Growth Mindset:** There is a growth mindset grounded in curiosity. Team members are aware of each other's strengths and weaknesses, and they seek feedback that will help them improve performance.

10. **Ownership:** The entire team feels a joint sense of ownership for their collective results, and they behave like owners.

Building High Performance Teams
Individuals play the game, but teams beat the odds

Whether you are a coach of a sports team, an emerging leader, or a CEO, these ten traits are vital. When a team exhibits them, it is firing on all cylinders. The chain is unbreakable. The outcome will be extraordinary results that fuel positive feelings and tangible rewards shared with respected comrades. I've been fortunate enough to serve on a few teams like this, and each ranks vividly on my list of most treasured memories.

Of course, I've also been on teams that did not perform so well. Perhaps you've been on a team that:

- Confronts tough issues in unproductive ways that damage team morale
- Tries to smooth over and "manage away" tough issues, rather than confronting them assertively
- Avoids contentious issues altogether, or waits for someone else to bring them up
- Settles for "adequate" solutions to tough, contentious problems, rather than staying with the tension to prompt innovative breakthroughs

These teams suffer from an inability to handle difficult challenges productively, one of the most common root causes of low-performing teams. A team has become problematic when it:

- Behaves in ways designed to lower the self-esteem of team members who don't agree
- Withholds information about the problem
- Focuses too quickly on one favored solution rather than on encouraging exploration of many possible ways of handling the problem
- Protects its own parochial interests rather than refocusing the team on the shared higher business purpose

- Devalues the potential contributions of others who look at the problem from a different angle, and seeks input only from those who think like they do
- Talks too much, and listens too little

So why do team members behave this way? Mostly it's because this is how they were taught to handle contentious issues by parents, caregivers, teachers, and other role models during their formative years.

Most of us learned two paradigms for dealing with stressful situations and confrontations:

Learned Paradigms	
Passive	*Aggressive*
• "I get along by going along." • "Don't rock the boat." • "It's important to be liked, and they'll like me more if I give in."	• "It's important to be a winner." • "If I win, then the other person must lose." • "It's important to be tough. If I change my position, I'll look weak, and I can't let that happen."

What can leaders do to move teams from low to high performance and get around unhelpful learned paradigms? The best leaders understand these paradigms and manage them proactively by modeling and teaching constructive contention. Specifically, they help their teams:

1. Maintain and build mutual self-esteem
   - Avoid attacks that threaten self-esteem

- Seek opportunities to reinforce teammates
- Catch, highlight, and reward constructive contention

2. Maximize information flow
   - Encourage extensive sharing of team knowledge about problems for purposes of growth
   - Seek deeper understanding and clarify by asking in-depth questions
   - Be open to other opinions, and accept that you cannot know everything
   - Listen deeply to fully understand an opposing point of view rather than immediately rebuffing it
   - Summarize what you have heard to ensure accuracy and show that you are listening

3. Foster creative solutions
   - Champion the curious and courageous because organizations often resist them because they dislike their disruptive prodding and probing
   - Welcome diversity in personal style and ideas
   - Seek different perspectives and encourage contrarian points of view
   - Go beyond the first solution and challenge solutions with alternatives

4. Find the higher business purpose
   - Avoid turf battles and parochial power plays
   - Proactively seek areas of common ground and shared business purpose
   - And my favorite: ask the question, "If our customers or consumers were here, what would they say?"

If you need to form a high performance team, give advance consideration to team chemistry and the ability of individual players to proactively deal with contention constructively. Here is my ten-step process for doing just that:

How to Build a High Performance Team

1. **Assess** individual strengths and behavioral preferences
2. **Select** members using a plan to complement strengths and fill gaps to achieve balance and synergy
3. Develop a charter, define roles, and **align** on the most important goals and rewards
4. Proactively **create an environment** in which teammates can learn about each other personally to better understand their formative life experiences, what drives them, and ultimately build trust
5. Establish a cadence of **team training** that incorporates real-world and mission critical challenges and obstacles
6. Define lead and lag success metrics as well as a process to **monitor progress**
7. Establish **feedback** mechanisms and norms for making decisions and holding one another **accountable**
8. Clarify needed **support** from stakeholders
9. Finalize rules of engagement and **execute**
10. **Course-correct** via team work sessions (See *The 4 Disciplines of Execution* by Chris McChesney, Sean Covey, and Jim Huling for an excellent model of this)

We all have individual strengths that enable us to perform certain roles and tasks more comfortably and better than others. Members of higher performing teams learn to lean on one another's strengths to synergistically achieve a higher level of performance than could be achieved by operating individually or in silos. They also understand that differences challenge assumptions, and assumptions are sometimes blind spots. Unbalanced teams will have more blind spots, more unproductive conflict, and more unforced errors. A great leader needs to constantly assess the balance the team is achieving and orchestrate it proactively.

Now let's take a look at a leader who did this with excellence.

A SUCCESS MODEL

I like to use analogies and metaphors to help crystallize a point, so let's look outside the business world for a success model. There are so many good examples of insight and inspiration when it comes to leaders of high-performing teams. The coxswain on a rowing crew, the conductor of an orchestra, the quarterback of a football team; the list goes on and on. All of these leaders can have an exponential impact on their teams if they fully grasp this leadership principle, pull the right levers, and push the right buttons.

I can think of no better place to look for inspiration than the most powerful leadership role in the world: the president of the United States of America. Abraham Lincoln's boldness in building a balanced and dynamic leadership team comprised of his rivals is well documented by Doris Kearns Goodwin in her award winning book, *A Team of Rivals*. But I'm using a more recent example. Many years ago, I wrote a paper for a class at Purdue University. The paper was titled *Leading with Character*, and the subject was Ronald Reagan. In my research I was introduced to the man who would become one of my heroes because of his extraordinary leadership.

When Ronald Reagan took the leadership reins as President, our economy was faltering. The rate of inflation had hit an alarming 13.5 percent, interest rates had ballooned to over 20 percent, unemployment exceeded 10 percent, and our foreign policy was a train wreck. Like many politicians, Ronald Reagan offered us hope during his campaign. Fortunately, he also brought leadership skills to turn hope into action that ultimately delivered sustained prosperity for our country. Whether you agreed with his ideology and political philosophies or not, you had to respect his leadership. He surrounded himself with a strong cadre of leaders willing to speak up and push back on their leader. Without a team that included leaders such as George Shultz, Jim Baker and Casper Weinberger, Ronald Reagan would not have been able to achieve what he did for our country.

President Reagan encouraged constructive contention that made his team stronger. He was secure enough to listen to his team and then make a call and accept responsibility for the results. He had the guts to do what he firmly believed was right, not just what was popular. (His successful handling of the air traffic controller crisis is a great example.) Reagan united people rather than dividing them to achieve power. He embraced his adversaries in a genuine attempt to find common ground and achieve progress, rather than arrogantly digging in his heels and blaming his adversaries for the paralysis rampant in Washington. His work with Tip O'Neill was a model for achieving progress even when faced with a formidable adversary with a conflicting agenda.

Ronald Reagan was one of the most successful presidents in the history of the United States of America because he built a synergistic team that beat the odds. In the face of significant adversity, he (and his team) dramatically improved our economy and strengthened our country's leadership position and role globally. Yes, he was a great communicator. But more importantly, he built and orchestrated a synergistic, high performance team that was much more powerful than the sum of its parts.

Chapter 3

Strategic Leadership

M any companies pay large sums of money to consultants to develop strategic plans. Sometimes I wish they would just donate those dollars to a worthy charity instead! The problem isn't that the strategic plans are bad *per se*, it's that the leaders and difference-makers who will be implementing the plans aren't involved enough in the analysis and building of the plans. Thus, their plans are largely outsourced, and they miss the opportunity to use the planning process to elevate workforce engagement, collaboration, alignment, innovation, accountability, and ownership of the plan itself. The outcome often doesn't live up to the hype. This gives strategic planning a bad name.

LEADERSHIP PRINCIPLE #3

Organizations inherently complicate things; servant leaders help their organizations focus on strategic priorities and simplify operations to accelerate progress.

THE LEADER'S CHALLENGE

It's well documented that the pace of change is accelerating. Long gone are the days when a three- or five-year strategic plan addressed reality even just a few months after its launch. It is harder than ever to align an entire organization with the fewer, bigger, and more market-meaningful ideas that might lead a company to prosperity.

In my work, I regularly hear leaders complain about the inability of their workforces to execute. I can empathize because I've been a CEO, and I've been tempted to do the same thing. But what if that's not the real root cause of the problem? Sometimes it's a case of leadership not doing everything it could to engage key leaders and difference-makers in the building of the plan and its deployment. The ultimate measure of a strategic plan is its effectiveness in helping everyone in an organization make tough choices that lead to sustainable growth. The goal is to get team-mates rowing together in the same direction like an efficient crew. But many strategic plans fail because they leave the door open to just about anything anybody wants to do.

In an attempt to focus the whole organization on goals and priorities, most leaders will cascade their list of priorities through-out the business. But if each layer of management adds its own set of priorities, employees are left to pick from a long list of pri-orities as they try to decide what deserves attention. Given this smorgasbord approach to leadership, people on the front lines of the business end up setting their own priorities independently, and the best practices of focus, alignment, engagement, and col-laboration cannot be fully achieved. It's like a rowing crew with the athletes rowing out of sync. And leaders subsequently wonder why the organization is so darned slow, why momentum is rarely achieved, and why performance against the original goals is less than optimal.

Research reveals that the effort to focus is a tough job. As noted earlier, most organizations are not effectively connecting their people to their goals in a way that is personally relevant, let alone motivating. The commitment gap between full-on employee engagement and mere job satisfaction is widening at a time when more and more people are seeking a higher sense of purpose and engagement in their work.

Strategies designed to drive profitable growth often require changes in human behavior. The data suggests that strategies that might have looked promising in the boardroom are not making their way to the front lines with the context and clarity required to drive workforce commitment. It is wishful thinking to expect workers to clairvoyantly lift themselves up from the daily grind and change their behavior without a significant amount of communication, context, and—above all—a motivating answer to the critical question, "How does my work help us win?"

Unfortunately, that is what is happening in many organizations.

WHAT MATTERS MOST

The founder, chairman, and CEO of a very successful family owned business told me when I first met him to discuss the future of his company that he and his company had no need for a strategic plan. He said, as he pointed to his head, "Besides, we already have a strategic plan, and it's right here!" But he was closing in on retirement and about to hand over the reigns of the family business to his children, who were fraught with uncertainty about the company's path forward and the roles each of them would play. They wanted my help, but their father clearly felt that a strategic plan was unnecessary for their successful business. I knew that he had been an accomplished football player and that he was a big fan of the local professional football team, so I asked him what he would think if the new head coach tried to coach the team without a playbook. This, along with some other examples, finally got his attention.

His original opinion about strategic planning is not unique. Many leaders are wary of—or even avoid—strategic planning because:

- It can be a colossal waste of time
- It can drain resources and shift focus away from critical priorities
- It is hard to do well
- It can be obsolete before it's even finished, given the increasing pace of change
- It seems unnecessary for many successful leaders who are inherently strategic, or at least successfully opportunistic

In fact, one of the most successful business leaders, Herb Kelleher of Southwest Airlines, once said, "We have a strategic plan, it's called *doing things*."

I'm a big fan of action too, and I dislike academic and theoretical exercises far removed from the realities of the front lines of business. I will be the first to admit that strategic plans are not cast in stone as they once were due to the rapid pace of innovation and change. However, every business needs a plan or road map for prosperity. Without one, the business is rudderless. What matters most now is a clear sense of purpose and strategic direction, grounded in shared core values. The founders of Google talk about having a strategic foundation that's rock solid, while having a plan that is fluid. I like that. I believe strategic

planning is an ongoing journey that should be integrated into
the business model and processed dynamically with agility, not
a one-time event.

When done well, strategic planning can be a:

- Catalyst for organizations trying to reach the next level
- Mechanism for driving focus and alignment behind a
  common corporate vision to fuel growth and improve
  operating results
- Roadmap to proactively address opportunities or challenges in an evolving marketplace
- Blueprint for firms looking to acquire or be acquired
- Living, breathing ongoing process for recognizing the
  quickening cadence between strategy and execution
- Differentiating tool that cultivates and tests talent, and
  helps leaders identify difference-makers and achieve a
  clearer view of future leadership succession

It's About the Planning, Not the Plan

As a general, Dwight D. Eisenhower was fond of saying, "It's
about the planning, not the plan." I couldn't agree more. Potential
clients often ask me why we can't just go offsite for a few days and
hammer out a strategic plan. I understand their sense of urgency
and desire for action, but many of the business building "aha
moments" and breakthroughs that I've seen over the years spring
from the cross-functional work sessions that happen when probing, analyzing, and building the plan collaboratively. It's about the
planning, not the plan.

When you mention the word "plan" to most people, they
think of something concrete such as a travel plan or a blueprint

used by builders. These plans identify a specific beginning and end with precise steps along the way. These plans are neat, prescribed, and manageable. You figure out what to do and then do it. But not all types of plans have that level of precision. In a fluid, unpredictable environment you need to have a very different understanding of plans and planning. In military strategy, this is well understood because leaders know that their strategy must withstand contact with the enemy. Similar to military strategy, business strategy should be developed and applied in an increasingly dynamic environment, and the distinction between planning and the plan is evermore relevant for senior executives charged with crafting a company's strategy and bringing out the best in their people.

In my work, I find that many leaders just want to check the strategic plan box and get on with the work at hand. Many that I encounter want to go off-site for a few days with colleagues, list all the problems, define the root causes, and agree to actions that will remedy their situation. I've heard many say, "We know what to do. We just need to lock ourselves in a room, make the plan, and get busy implementing it."

In some cases, their expectations of what can be achieved with a strategic plan are unrealistic. The model in their mind is more like a blueprint for a house or building. They anticipate that by doing the necessary analysis and writing down how their business will succeed, the world will be converted from uncertain to certain. In their eyes, the strategic plan becomes a device for control rather than one of guidance and inspiration. But successful strategic planning is not about controlling. It's about unleashing the collaborative and innovative spirit of the people you lead by focusing them collectively in such a way that their energy and effort will fuel sustained growth, much like the forementioned coxswain focuses a rowing crew.

Leaders who want to use strategic planning merely to fix the persistent ambiguity and uncertainty their business faces will be disappointed. When, inevitably, a plan does not predict the future with perfection, this can manifest into the mistaken belief that strategic planning is a colossal waste of time and resources. Leaders then find themselves simply ignoring any document that has been produced, and their followers lose faith in the ability of their leaders.

As I look back over my many years creating strategic plans, I recognize that none were close to perfect or clairvoyant. Still, I encourage leaders to think of the plan as a guidance tool, and to focus on the planning *process* itself as the engine and fuel for the sustained growth they desire. It's a mechanism for bringing out the best in the people they lead, and seeing which of their leaders will step up and which leaders will step back. As many athletes have learned, most of the joy and fulfillment is in the journey, not at the finish line. I also remind impatient leaders that we will not wait until the strategic plan is finalized to take action. By the time the plan is fully developed and rolled out to their entire company, we are already knee deep in the implementation of the ah-ha ideas and actions that emanate throughout the strategic planning process.

Servant leaders avoid the strategic planning trap of simply summarizing everything that is going on in the business today, and then putting the plan on the shelf. That is a colossal waste of everyone's time.

The best strategic plans drive tough choices and accountability deeper into the organization, focusing resources where they create the most economic value. Remember, the best plans are:

- Balanced, holistic and long-term
- Developed collaboratively by the entire leadership team with broad input
- Built around a shared and well-communicated vision and stakeholder principles
- Disruptive, provocative, and an incubator of big business building ideas
- Based on clear assessments of the organization and the dynamics of the market
- Balanced cross-functionally and aligned across business units and lines of business
- Driven down to focused goals and performance measures that will become the roadmap for accountable execution
- Accomplished in a manner that builds a shared vision, ownership and cohesiveness
- Explicit and well communicated—answers the question: what does it mean to me?
- Ingrained into the fabric of the organization as a dynamic core business practice that helps keep the company continually focused on its strategic direction

Strategy Built on Vision, Mission, and Values

The fundamental purpose of strategic planning is to align a company's vision and mission with its core values, and to chart a path forward that will deliver desired results over a sustained period of time. This is the strategic foundation. Without alignment on vision, mission and values, planning lacks a stable foundation. Vision defines the destination. Mission includes everything needed to make it a reality—including your core values, purpose, the promise you make to your customers and stakeholders, the reasons to believe that promise, and your strategic plan for successful execution. Core values are important because they, along with your organization's core strengths, provide a sturdy foundation upon which to build growth strategies, tactics, and, ultimately, the execution and actions that will deliver desired results. The strategic plan is the roadmap that helps leaders and their teams navigate the journey, *but the planning process itself is where the real magic happens.* (More about this later.)

Even if your organization already has well-defined vision, mission, and core values statements, they should be reviewed and used as guideposts throughout the strategic planning process. Don't assume that every member of a team can articulate the company's vision, mission, and core values. Based on my experience, most cannot, which is why I recommend beginning with the building of this important strategic foundation. Even if everyone has these statements committed to memory, you must ensure they are current, that they truly resonate with stakeholders and team members, and that your team is resolutely aligned with them.

One of the most important aspects of any successful strategic planning process is the amount of time and energy invested in probing and testing for alignment on this important foundation. This is because most plans fall apart, much like a crumbling building, when times get tough. Stress factors can ultimately compromise plans that were built on faulty and misaligned foundations. As management guru Peter Drucker once said, culture eats strategy for breakfast.

Any successful strategic planning process should include deep-dive analyses and multiple work sessions with the core leadership team in which they objectively and honestly assess their organization's strengths, weaknesses, opportunities, and threats (SWOT). See the flow chart on page 31 for how it all comes together.

Building the Foundation

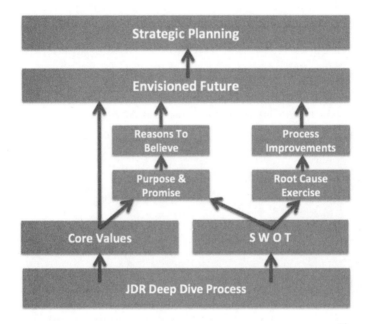

Vision

A statement of your vision for the future helps your organization by painting a vivid picture of the success you hope to achieve. It is the inspirational articulation of your organization's dreams and hopes. It reminds everyone of what you are trying to achieve and build, and where your strategic plan needs to take you. While this vision statement doesn't detail how you're going to get there, it does set the direction for strategic and operational planning. When creating a vision statement, it's important to unlock the imagination of your team and dare to dream big. This is because your vision statement should capture the imagination and passion of your organization by articulating an aspirational destination.

Mission

A vital element of a company's mission statement is its fundamental purpose for existing *beyond making money*. The purpose should be engaging and somewhat idealistic, and it should reach beyond typical business goals. The secret to creating a great statement of purpose is to focus on why your organization exists at an existential level, not simply the products and services your organization provides. While some might view this as unimportant, a Gallup study found that customers who are aligned with a brand or company's purpose give that company twice as much share of wallet as customers who are not aligned.

Southwest Airlines and CVS are great examples of companies with strong purpose statements that helped them stay the course through strategic challenges. When most airlines started charging passengers for checking bags, Southwest fell back upon its purpose statement of "To connect people to what is important in their lives through friendly, reliable and low-cost air travel." They decided to *not* charge their customers for checking bags, and made this decision part of a marketing campaign, leveraging it as yet another example of how they uniquely serve their customers.

Similarly, CVS leaned into its purpose of "helping people on their path to better health" when they decided to discontinue the sale of tobacco products. While they lost short term sales and profits that were fueled by tobacco products, the longer term research showed that consumers were five times more likely to shop at CVS once they learned about this choice.

Once you have identified a unique, compelling, and aspirational purpose, it's time to articulate a succinct promise and the reasons to believe the promise. Ask yourself: what promise do you make to your most important consumers and/or customers? What are the most persuasive reasons for them to believe that you can deliver on that promise uniquely, or at least better than anyone else?

Core Values

Core values are traits or intrinsic qualities that are considered worthwhile to your people and your stakeholders, and they should represent the bedrock of your culture. They should be deeply held convictions. For companies, they are statements about how the organization will value their associates, customers, business partners, and stakeholders. Strong statements of core values describe character-based principles and actions that are innate to the core values held by most individuals within an organization. These collective values meld together to form your company's culture. If you think about your own life, your values should form the cornerstones for all that you do. If you are living true to your values, then they define where you spend your time and energy. The same should be true for your organization.

Objectives, Goals, Strategies, and Measures (OGSM)

Objectives, goals, strategies, and measures define the roadmap your team will use to move your organization from where it is today to the desired vision you have articulated. They specifically define who will accomplish what and by when. They must never simply be a summary of what is going on in your organization today, or the entire planning process will be a waste of time.

Once the core leadership team builds its strategic foundation, it's time to craft the objectives, goals, strategies, and measures (OGSM) by strategic vector. Strategic vectors are functions, roles, or vital stakeholders. Examples of strategic vectors include consumer (marketing), customer (sales), operations, supply chain, IT, finance, and so on. The leaders of each vector will play vital roles as you build the plan, and a sound strategic planning process will help them learn, grow, and force-multiply their leadership and collaborative influence. For the leader of the organization, this process can also be a great test to see which leaders are going to embrace transformational change and step up, and which will step back.

Use Strategic Planning to Force-Multiply

How do leaders get their workforce strategically aligned on the truly important issues and fired up about raising the bar? If leaders want a performance-based culture of collaboration and innovation where people are truly committed to the company's success, they must help each and every person feel like they are personally important and connected to something that truly matters. For leaders who fully grasp the importance of their servant role to the people they lead, a collaborative strategic planning process can be a robust vehicle for establishing the roots of engagement needed to raise the bar, bring out the best in the people they lead, and drive sustained growth. Servant leaders on the team will embrace this role, while those more self-interested and less focused on bringing out the best in others will likely struggle with it and step back.

Obviously, thorough analytics and insightful strategic thinking are important when developing a plan. But even in companies that invest significant resources developing a very smart plan, leaders often under-invest in the work required to elevate workforce engagement to the level needed to achieve their company's full potential. I've seen very good strategic plans result in mediocre or even poor results because the plan was not executed by an aligned and committed workforce. Conversely, I've seen mediocre plans deliver outstanding results because the people executing the plans were aligned and committed to success.

Strategic planning doesn't have to be, nor should it be, an ivory tower exercise. Instead, it should be a springboard for the collaboration and innovation needed to drive improved results. Key difference-makers throughout the organization must be engaged. I like to use a core leadership team to do the bulk of the planning, but also encourage these leaders to force-multiply their influence by forming and leading their own sub-team of difference-makers to help build the plan iteratively and with broader input. These sub-teams help the core leadership team search for blind spots that they are missing because they are not as close to the front lines. They also stir collaboration and engagement among the troops—who always appreciate being asked to help. Ultimately, they lead to a better, more informed plan that benefits from more broad-scale ownership throughout the company once the plan is executed.

This process takes time to work correctly, and should not be rushed. Team members need to go back and forth from their day jobs and their team's work sessions to analyze and test-drive new insights and ideas, and the objectives, goals, strategies, and measures discussed below. The sub-teams should also be encouraged to reach deeper into the organization for feedback to ensure they are not missing something critical that could hamstring execution if ignored in the planning process. Engagement should be intentionally cultivated from the beginning of the planning process, and *not* simply when the plan is finished and launched.

On several occasions, I have seen sub-teams uncover challenges and opportunities that were previously unrecognized by the core leadership team. When orchestrated well, this process can yield a more robust strategic plan, and fuel a more energized workforce eager to execute the plan like an owner rather than merely an employee. Here are a few examples where sub-teams made a difference:

- Recommended changes to a stage gate product development process that accelerated new product development and commercialization by solving dilemmas to which the leadership team was unaware.
- Identified a plethora of supply chain opportunities to simplify operations, consolidate vendors, reduce SKUs, shrink inventory, and improve customer service.
- Shined a light on behaviors inconsistent with the core values of the company, leading to the outplacement of leaders who were hamstringing the performance of the company.
- Crafted a plan to improve their company's website, re-engineered the e-commerce platform and improved the effectiveness of their company's digital marketing efforts.
- Highlighted problems with their company's sales force compensation plan and recommended changes that ultimately fueled increased sales.
- Identified the need for more training and leadership development at their company, recommended a new plan, and managed execution that led to improved retention of higher performing employees and lowered recruiting expenses.
- Uncovered multiple occasions of fraud within the company and made recommendations to remedy.
- Helped the owners and the board of directors realize that there was no viable long-term succession plan for continued family leadership of the company. This led to significant changes to roles and responsibilities on the senior leadership team that transformed the company.

Launching Sub-Teams

Once the core team has established the strategic foundation

detailed above, it's time to form and launch sub-teams to help the leader of each strategic vector begin the strategic planning process. Below are a few tips for success.

Team Construction Criteria

1. **Size:** 4–10 members
2. **Complementary abilities and behavior:** Build a synergistic team that is more powerful than the sum of its parts by being attentive to the strengths and weaknesses of each member.
3. **Commitment:** Choose members that you are sure will step up to the plate.
4. **Development:** Use this work as an opportunity to develop difference-makers. Serving on a sub-team could be an opportunity to provide a stretch assignment to a key retention employee who has been itching to make a bigger contribution.
5. **Cross-fertilization and networking:** Choose members capable of reaching out into the organization and networking to gain needed insight and alignment across a broad range of functions within the company, as well as external business partners.
6. **Alignment:** Confirm membership with the core team leader before launching to help ensure a well-balanced approach to the strategic planning process across the company.

Team Initiation and Launch Steps

Use key materials from the most recent core leadership team work session to educate sub-team members on purpose and process, and give them context for change. Feel free to tailor your message and direction to the sub-team to your individual communication style and the unique needs of your team.

1. Make it clear up front that we are not trying to "boil the ocean." The work must focus on what matters most and what will have the biggest impact on results.

2. Leverage this work as an opportunity to elevate commitment to the company by stressing the importance of this initiative and how important team members are to future success. Most emerging leaders will welcome this opportunity and view it as a very positive step.

3. Communicate to your team that they will be expected to reach outside and into the organization for insight and feedback occasionally. Work with your team to create a list of difference-makers in your sphere of influence (and preferably outside your function) that you can tap into as the project progresses. The goal is to challenge assumptions that might be blind spots.

4. Review the principles of constructive contention (see Chapter 2) with your team and encourage a candid discussion about how the team plans to operate to maximize success.

5. Review the output from the previous core leadership team work session with your sub-team, seeking their input on items the core leadership team might have missed.

6. Record sub-team questions and feedback for sharing with the core team for purposes of growth, alignment, and follow-up.

Before diving into the drafting of objectives, goals, strategies, and measures, each sub-team leader should provide their sub-team with the perspective and context they need to maximize their contributions. They should share the heretofore work of the core leadership team in the establishment of the strategic foundation. I encourage sub-team leaders to have their teams challenge and kick around the work of the core team to find opportunities for improvement that she can then take back to the core team for consideration.

Once this is accomplished, the sub-team leader works with his team to further analyze their current situation (the situation review) beginning with a SWOT (strengths, weaknesses, opportunities and threats) analysis and then diving deeper where further marketplace or company data and analysis are required.

	Helpful To Achieving Goals	Harmful To Achieving Goals
Internal Origin Attributes of the organization	**Strengths**	**Weaknesses**
External Origin Attributes of the environment	**Opportunities**	**Threats**

Strengths	Weaknesses
GOOD NOW Maintain Build Leverage	**BAD NOW** Remedy Stop

Opportunities	Threats
GOOD FUTURE Prioritize Invest Accelerate Optimize	**BAD FUTURE** Counter Crush Avoid

Once this situation review is completed, the team works to define the strategic implications of their conclusions and key findings. I also encourage leaders to engage their teams in brainstorming about their dreams for the future, which I call the *envisioned future*. Together, the situation review, the strategic implications, and the envisioned future form the platform for development of the objectives, goals, strategies, and measures in the strategic plan.

Roadmap to a Strategic Plan

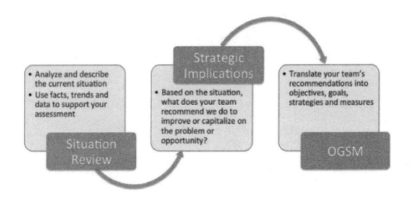

- Analyze and describe the current situation
- Use facts, trends and data to support your assessment

Situation Review

Strategic Implications

- Based on the situation, what does your team recommend we do to improve or capitalize on the problem or opportunity?

- Translate your team's recommendations into objectives, goals, strategies and measures

OGSM

Objectives

An objective is a qualitative statement of what the organization wants to achieve. Essentially, objectives translate the longer-term envisioned future into something more concrete for specific areas of the company, or strategic vectors. For some organizations, objectives might not change for several years. For others—like those in rapidly changing industries—objectives may change more frequently. While the envisioned future looks out over the next five to ten years, the objectives detail what must happen over the next one to three years to make the envisioned future a reality. A good way to test if you have landed on an objective is to keep asking "*Why?*" The answer will often ladder you up to a more meaningful objective. Also, if it describes *how* you will achieve the envisioned future, it belongs in the strategy portion of the strategic plan, and is not an objective.

Examples of Objectives:
- Grow the humor segment of the greeting card market, and increase our share of that growing segment
- Build a stronger relationship with key school administrators that leads to increased sales
- Deliver better customer service than anyone in the industry
- Build a stronger organization, both organically and with new talent
- Meet stakeholders' sales and profit expectations

Goals

A goal is a quantitative statement of what you want to achieve. Most goals begin with an active verb such as "increase" or "decrease" and define the amount of improvement required. For example, for a company with an objective of becoming a top rated employer, goals might include increasing employee satisfaction, increasing employee trust of leadership, and decreasing employee turnover, all by a specified amount (the measures can be more specifically defined in the measures section below). Again, if it describes *how* you are going to do it, it is not a goal.

Examples of Goals:
- Extend our leadership position in the glass cleaner category, growing market share to 65 percent in two years.

- Reduce the time it takes us to achieve 80 percent ACV distribution from twelve weeks to eight weeks after first ship date.
- Grow the percentage of sales generated by new products launched within the previous three years to more than 25 percent in three years.
- Reduce gross-to-net sales deductions from 5.2 percent to 3.8 percent in four years.
- Steadily decrease SG&A as a percentage of net sales over time.

Strategies

Strategies are the heart and soul of any strategic plan. They describe *how* you are going to accomplish your goals, and include details of a general approach or methodology. For example, a strategy to increase employee satisfaction might be to implement more flexible work programs.

Examples of Strategies:
- Extend our brand equity and expansion-joint capabilities to adjacent markets.
- Field targeted marketing programs to fuel awareness and trial of our new product, and generate enough incremental sales to pay back the investment within eighteen months.
- Use fact-based selling to convince customers that they are missing growth opportunities.
- Re-engineer the new product development process to fail faster on bad ideas, lower the cost of experimentation, and improve the success rate of new products launched.
- Acquire niche companies that are synergistic with our competencies and cost structure, and accretive to profit margins.

- Develop, launch, and manage a talent development program to increase supervisor accountability for coaching and developing the people they lead.

Measures

Measures help ensure balance and accountability in the execution of the strategic plan. Whether you call them measures, metrics, or KPIs (key performance indicators) is unimportant. What *is* important is that they be a time-bound statement of what success looks like. Measures should provide the foundation for a balanced scorecard to track progress and ensure appropriate course-correction and resource allocation as you navigate your strategic plan. This scorecard should gauge the overall health of your organization and provide real-time feedback on your organization's progress achieving the growth you desire. It should tell you where you are right now relative to the destination you have stated in your vision, objectives, and goals. Ultimately, this scorecard of measures is the tool your team uses to hold itself accountable, and should therefore connect directly to your incentive compensation and rewards programs.

Examples of Measures:
- Market share by year (or some other time period).
- Talent metrics such as employee engagement, measured using employee surveys—not just top-down assessment.
- Consumer metrics such as awareness, acquisition, conversion, usage, and brand equity.
- P&L measures such as sales, cost of goods sold (COGS), gross profit margin, SG&A, operating margin, EBITDA, and all of these measures as a percentage of net sales.
- Steadily increasing percentage of sales coming from new products launched over a defined period of time.

- Metrics designed to monitor the health of the base/core business.
- Balance sheet measures such as cash flow, working capital, CAPEX, ROCE, etc.
- Operational metrics such as lines on time complete, throughput, COGS savings, etc.
- Customer service metrics such as net promoter score.
- Leading indicator measures (lead measures) that might provide early warning signals to course-correct before it's too late to improve your results (lag measures).

As I mentioned earlier, this process takes time. But that does not mean the team has to wait until the plan is finalized to take action on challenges and solutions identified during the planning process that the entire team agrees should be addressed immediately.

Once the strategic plan—including objectives, goals, strategies, and measures—has been drafted, the team works collaboratively and iteratively across strategic vectors to ensure alignment, coordination, and synergy. At this point, I also like to step into execution to test-drive the strategic plan before fully executing it. Each strategic vector leader should work with her sub-team to assess the capacity and capabilities of the organization to execute the plan with excellence. Specifically, each team assesses and rates its current capabilities on a scale of 1–5 with 1=poor and 5=excellent. Then it recommends actions that will improve its organization to level 5. The team details the resources required to make it happen, searches for lower value work that can be eliminated or at least reallocated to higher value work, and designates a leader for each action. Once this assessment is completed, it is used as a stepping stone toward a three year action plan that details more specific actions required to execute the strategic plan, as you can see in the diagram below. These last two steps invariably cause the team to reconsider its strategic plan, focus it on what matters most, and make a few adjustments before it is locked in and launched. Finally, I recommend dusting off the root cause analysis performed earlier in the process and using it as a process or gut-check to ensure nothing of significance was missed.

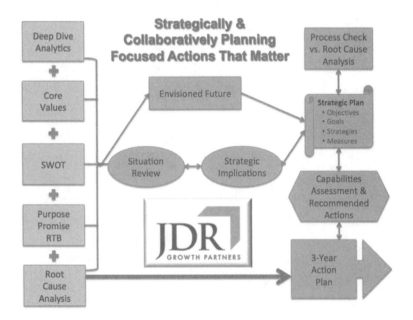

Some more aggressive and action-oriented leaders will look at this strategic planning method and suggest that it is cumbersome and consumes too much time, obviously a precious resource. They would rather go off-site for a couple of days, identify all the problems and challenges their team faces, determine the root causes, detail the actions needed to remedy the situation, and get back to work and get it done. They might even call this a strategic plan. But these are plans built on a foundation of weaknesses rather than strengths and core values. This approach could lead to some improved results, but it only scratches the surface. By urgently following the bold line in the chart on page 45, they miss out on the many opportunities for their team to learn, challenge, debate, collaborate, innovate, harmonize, bond and achieve true alignment on the path forward. Within six months their team is often right back to where they were before, looking a lot like that out-of-sync rowing crew I alluded to earlier.

When a leadership team embarks on a strategic planning process, their work will be socialized at lightning speed. As this happens, be ready for the workforce to be increasingly distracted by rumors, wondering what this might mean for them. Servant leaders have the emotional intelligence to realize that people don't fear change—they fear loss. Leaders should not only control the message, they should leverage it by proactively and transparently communicating what they are up to, even when they don't have all the answers. (More about this in Chapter 6.) Candor fuels employee engagement because people want to know that their leaders are doing their jobs. They also want to know that their leaders care enough about them to include them in planning the company's future. When managed proactively, leaders can use this process to drive commitment and ultimately improved results. That's much better than the uninspiring experience we've all had when we received a new company vision and strategic plan delivered to us from the ivory tower, only to file it and never reference it again.

I encourage leaders to seek out and encourage constructive contention throughout this entire strategic planning process because it often uncovers the root causes of the biggest problems that can hamstring growth. Further, when constructive contention is orchestrated positively, it can lead to solutions and exciting new opportunities.

Servant leaders force-multiply the power of constructive contention.

I also encourage leaders to push to the end, fully documenting plans complete with roles, responsibilities, measures, and signatures—even though the plan will evolve over time. There are two reasons I recommend this. The first is to surface disagreements that may otherwise remain hidden. You can have all the discussions you like with your teammates and associates and think that your leadership team is in agreement . . . until you actually distill these discussions into a written document that people have to sign. It's in the crafting of your organization's position that you might realize that you're *not* all on the same page. The second reason is that it provides a platform from which change can be leveraged. This line-in-the-sand approach may seem paradoxical, but the very process of preparing the plan has you thinking about the future, making the tough choices that were previously glossed over during the daily grind, and re-allocating resources away from inefficiencies and toward growth. While the plan itself and the planners needed to be flexible and adaptable, this linear and disciplined process will generate preparedness, drive accountability, and ultimately fuel results because it brings out the best in the people you lead. Most importantly, the impact on the people you lead and your organization will be lasting if you stay the course.

Execution and Accountability

Remember, the desire for perfection is often the enemy of progress, and the strategic plan is a work in progress. It's not a set-and-forget instrument. It's a living and breathing document that *guides* alignment and collaboration and helps people in your organization make tough choices. When managers talk about "giving up on strategic planning," they haven't thought through how to keep their plan fresh. The fact that circumstances are changing rapidly is a very good reason to visit the plan regularly. How regularly? This varies by industry, of course, but I believe the plan should be worked on a monthly basis by the leadership team in work sessions where the agenda is defined by the strategic plan. The leader of each strategic vector owns his portion of the agenda each month so it is not just the CEO's or overall team leader's agenda. This one day per month becomes a strategic bucket into which leaders can dump topics related to the plan that are strategic but not urgent. I find this helps the team eliminate other meetings from the calendar, and this one day per month can become a very productive, roll-up-your-sleeves yet strategic day in which the team continues and even accelerates the momentum they generated in the strategic planning process. For more insight regarding execution of a plan, I highly recommend the book "*The 4 Disciplines of Execution*" by Chris McChesney, Sean Covey, and Jim Huling.

Organizational Structure, Roles, and Responsibilities

During the strategic planning process, many of my clients discover that their company is not organized optimally to achieve their vision and purpose. The strategic plan can be an excellent springboard to reorganizing structure, roles, and responsibilities. Here is my twelve-step process for syncing your organizational structure and capabilities with your vision, mission, core values, and strategic plan:

1. Review your company's purpose, promise, "reasons to believe," and your core values.
2. Prioritize the Goals in your strategic plan (OGSM) accordingly.

3. Prioritize the Actions in the 3-Year Action Plan accordingly. If you are looking for criteria for establishing priorities, refer back to the purpose, promise, and reasons to believe and assess the impact or value each specific goal or action will contribute to this statement of your intentions and strategic direction. Also, consider the degree of difficulty. I suggest using a five point scale, and plotting both impact and degree of difficulty on a two-dimensional X:Y chart.

4. Consider the more important day-to-day tasks that must be accomplished to run the business that might not be included in the OGSM or three-Year Action Plan. *Focus* on the most important tasks and prioritize them. Don't try to boil the ocean.

5. List key decisions that must be made starting with the highest priorities. To do this, process-map the workflow using decision trees for the most important actions, priorities, and tasks. Highlight key decisions, as well as who makes them today. Work with your team to simplify, streamline, re-engineer, and improve the effectiveness and efficiency of your decision-making. All of this should be grounded in an objective view of the current state and the root causes of less-than-optimal performance.

6. Identify touch points between strategic vectors/functions. How much value does each touch point add to the decision making process? Keep challenging why you do what you do today, looking beyond symptoms (effect) for root causes. Which steps or touch points could be eliminated, reduced, or reallocated to a more effective or efficient function or teammate? Which touch points add the most value, and which add little? Are we missing touch points that could improve the effectiveness or

efficiency of our decision-making? Seek cross-functional feedback to complement your thinking and augment potential blind spots.

7. Identify capabilities or skills we possess that are strengths we can lean on and leverage to get better.

8. What capabilities or skills need to be built or elevated to improve the effectiveness and efficiency of our decision-making, workflow, and the quality of our work? Be honest about the weaknesses we should augment with new talent or outside help.

9. Now, step back and examine your current organization today. Seek inefficiencies in the way we currently work in light of steps 1 through 8 above. Also, where do we need to improve our capabilities or invest resources to raise our game?

10. With this as your springboard, design at least one alternative organization structure that could help your organization improve your ability to deliver your stated purpose and promise that you make to your customers, and help you achieve the goals you've identified in your strategic plan. Once designed, draft the unique responsibilities and value-add for each function and role, highlighting changes versus the existing structure and roles.

11. Finally, test-drive the new organizational structure(s) and roles by repeating steps 5 through 8 above. Iterate modifications to improve the structure and roles further. Keep an eye out for hidden processes that would have to be changed to avoid something important slipping between the cracks once you transition into execution. Seek different points of view to challenge your thinking.

12. Assess your current talent, and deploy everyone where they add the most unique value by leveraging their strengths.

Ensure that difference-makers are differentiated, stretched, and placed in vital roles that will develop them into servant leaders. Use this as an opportunity to either commit to developing weaker talent, or outplace them gracefully. Begin recruiting immediately to fill skill gaps and strengthen your team.

People and Process

That last step takes us right back to chapters one and two. The best way for you to ensure that your strategy translates into execution that delivers desirable results is to sweat the details of people and process. Below I offer ten steps to better execution with several questions designed to help you improve the deployment of your people and the processes needed to execute your strategic plan with excellence.

1. Does your organizational structure alleviate or add unnecessary friction or barriers to your people executing effectively? Is your structure hamstringing your ability to achieve more? Are you investing appropriately into the talent needed to achieve your goals?

2. Do you honestly and consistently assess your talent and capabilities? When was the last time you did a complete talent review (not just appraisals) of your entire team or organization? Have you identified your difference-makers? Do you differentiate? Do you have the right talent and skills in critical roles?

3. Do you fully understand your culture? What are the values, mindset and attitudinal disposition of the people in key roles? Do their hearts, minds and aspirations align with leadership's vision for the organization?

4. Do you have a shortage of leadership? Are you cultivating future leaders? Are your current leaders in the organization encouraged and rewarded for developing future leaders?

5. Are you developing talent and systems in such a way where you don't need to rely too heavily on too few difference-makers to drive your business? Do you hold leaders accountable for improving the performance of all of the people they lead? Do you give poor performers the help they need to improve, and prune them if they cannot improve?

6. Do your people fully understand your envisioned future? Have you adequately communicated the strategic plan to achieve that vision? Do you keep it alive and compelling? Have you defined the precise activities and the behaviors required to achieve the goals in your strategic plan? Have you communicated clearly how these activities and behaviors will fuel your ability to accomplish your goals and achieve our vision?

7. Does each person know which activities and behaviors for which they are accountable, and why based on the markets you serve? And do they know how their responsibilities connect to the interdependent roles of teammates across the organization?

8. Do you have a system in place to measure the precise activities needed to deliver the strategic plan? Do you have a scorecard? Do you hold each other accountable for results? Do you regularly review, calibrate and course-correct your activities and behaviors based on new learning? Are you adequately focused on the consumers and customers you serve? Do you encourage and embrace constructive contention to foster continuous improvement, agility, innovation and growth?

9. Does your performance management and talent development process align coaching, training and development to the right behaviors and activities needed to achieve your goals and vision?
10. Are you rewarding and incentivizing the right activities and behaviors needed to drive the results you desire?

Leading your team across the bridge to growth requires both insightful strategy and improved execution. But as I said in the introduction to this book, there is a third ingredient too often overlooked: servant leadership. While strategy is important, servant leaders understand that achieving improved execution and results is first and foremost a people problem, not just a strategy problem.

A SUCCESS MODEL

I try to eat fairly healthy. But occasionally when I want to indulge in something really tasty, I head to Popeye's Louisiana Kitchen for spicy chicken, red beans and rice, and a biscuit. As a consumer, I have been a fan of Popeye's for many years. Unfortunately, Popeye's business was on the decline until Cheryl Bachelder was hired as the new CEO in 2007 to turn the company around. The stock price had declined by roughly 60 percent because of a long-term decline in sales and profits. Guest visits were declining at an alarming rate, and relations between corporate leaders and franchise owners were adversarial at best.

Cheryl and her team introduced the organization to the concept of servant leadership and focused the company first and foremost on their purpose and principles. They prioritized serving their franchisees and customers with excellence, and they measured their results with the highest levels of rigor and accountability. Cheryl and her team genuinely valued and prioritized the people they served both inside and outside of the organization. They understood that the best leaders have motives that go beyond self-interest—they serve a purpose greater than themselves—and they serve others well. They challenge the people they lead to pursue daring, bold aspirations, which grow the capabilities and confidence of the organization they lead. They shun the spotlight and instead shine it on the results of others. In doing so, they create a healthier work environment that ultimately produces better results.

By the end of calendar 2016, Popeye's average restaurant was up 45 percent in sales and profits. The stock price reached all-time highs. If you are interested in learning more about Cheryl's servant leadership approach and results, I highly recommend her book *Dare to Serve*.

I also want to highlight Walmart as a success model for this principle. Since Sam Walton founded the company in 1962, Walmart has been clear about its purpose as an organization. Of course, no company is perfect, but, for the most part, the people of the Walmart organization have been unwavering in their embrace of principles and core values. Equally important, Walmart has relentlessly focused its entire organization on a few big and simple goals that everyone, including its business partners, understands, because Walmart focuses so much energy on managing the details of execution relentlessly.

Walmart has lost some of its luster recently as consumer purchases migrate online, and e-tailers such as Amazon threaten its business model. But Walmart remains one of the most amazing success stories in the history of business. The growth in market capitalization and stock trend over the past thirty-four years speaks for itself.

Over the course of my career, Walmart has often been an important customer. On multiple occasions, a company I worked for won the Walmart Supplier of the Year award. I've travelled to Bentonville, Arkansas, more than any other city in the world, and I've attended the Walmart annual meeting with business partners and suppliers on several occasions.

Many times I've observed other business leaders mocking the down-home simplicity and down-to-earth nature of Walmart's culture. They do so at their own risk. Some manufacturers dislike Walmart because Walmart exposes flaws in their business models, and Walmart passes along savings from the inefficiencies that are uncovered to consumers or to its own bottom line. But the free market works. Walmart has made most of its business partners improve as a result of working with Walmart. The focus on wowing consumers with lower prices is almost cult-like—it's a strong mantra at the annual meeting, within the walls at headquarters, and in Walmart stores. Meetings at the Walmart offices have always been legendarily challenging for visitors. But over time, people have come to realize that this is a company that is dedicated and aligned throughout its massive organization to providing the most affordable products to shoppers to make their lives better, and Walmart will do whatever it takes to make that happen. You have to admire the focus, determination, and simplicity with which Walmart has executed its strategy. Of course, we'll see if they can navigate the digital transformation currently challenging their business model with the same level of success, but the success of their strategic focus over the last 50-plus years is undeniable.

Strategic companies such as Walmart make their strategies more executable because they say "no" a lot, and when they say "yes" it's a *big* yes. They fail fast on bad ideas, lower the cost of experimentation, and they focus precious resources on fewer, bigger, more consumer-meaningful ideas that generate the largest return on investment. Perhaps most importantly, they do the hard work required to achieve exceptional execution throughout their entire organization and with their business partners by engaging them in the planning process to ensure broad scale alignment and ownership of the plan. They've also won a lot more than they have lost.

Part Two

The Heavy Lifting

Chapter 4

Consumers and Customers Matter Most

Gravity is a powerful force of nature. The center of gravity is the point at which all of the weight of an object appears to be concentrated. It has a lot to do with the balance of forces, and this is similar to leadership. Leadership is a powerful force when focused in the right places and administered with the proper touch. Leaders have enormous influence on the center of gravity of their organizations. Where is it today? Where should it be? The best leaders realize it should be in the field with customers, consumers, and their troops who serve them.

LEADERSHIP PRINCIPLE #4
Champion the people who purchase and use your products and services; otherwise, corporate inertia will divert too much energy toward lower value work.

THE LEADER'S CHALLENGE
In many organizations, important decisions are made in conference rooms that do not include seats at the table for the most important people. Consumers and customers are not in the room! Consumer

research is occasionally cited to support an opinion or a recommendation, or comments from the field sales force are added to the discussion through a third party, but the focus of most of these conference-room conversations is still directed inward, not outward. Objectivity can be sacrificed, and this often leads to execution that falls short of delighting consumers and maximizing ROI (return on investment).

A leader can shift an organization's center of gravity by championing consumers and customers throughout the day. It's not easy because daily corporate demands steal time and energy. Leaders are busy managing stakeholders, handling urgent organizational fire drills, performing administrative duties, reviewing financial performance and projections, and so on. But there is a cause and effect relationship here. Without the former, all of the latter will ultimately suffer.

Most leaders talk about superior customer service and delighting consumers. But when you look deep into their organizations, you see behaviors misaligned with their words. People come to work every morning to the same job with mounting distractions, and it's easy to lose sight of what is best for the people who buy and use the company's products and services. It is human nature for workers to bias analysis, decisions, and behavior to self-interest instead of consumer or customer interests.

It's leadership's job to align individual, organizational, customer, and consumer interests as much as possible. Complete alignment may never be fully achieved, but it's a worthy goal. Research suggests that alignment is well below 50 percent in most organizations. The best leaders recognize this reality, and they work tirelessly to close the alignment gap.

WHAT MATTERS MOST

How can leaders shift the center of gravity externally? By walking the talk! It's important for leaders to get out of the corner office and model the behavior they want their organization to emulate. Ask the penetrating questions that remind your people that consumers and customers matter most. For example, begin every town hall or company-wide meeting with compelling stories about your consumers and customers. Bring the external world inside your company's walls, and *show* your people the value your organization adds to society.

Servant leaders focus their organization externally on the marketplace.

The best leaders visit the front lines regularly, particularly when they can add unique value to customer conversations and develop productive relationships with customers. They also attend ethnographic research sessions to actually *experience* their products and services with consumers in *their* world, real-time and elbow-to-elbow. To be clear, I am not suggesting that leaders should micro-manage or usurp the responsibilities of their marketing and sales teams. I'm recommending that leaders routinely join marketing and sales people in the field in order to become the champion of the customers and consumers they serve. Leaders who follow this advice will ultimately be more informed decision makers when they are back inside the walls of their companies, and they will teach their workforces how to make smarter choices.

Obviously, every leader's time is limited. Therefore, prioritization is key. I have found the simple customer strategy matrix on the next page to be an effective tool for fueling constructive debate regarding how to allocate precious resources and time to your customers. Each circle represents a customer. The size of each circle represents the profits generated with this customer over the trailing twelve months (TTM). The x-axis represents sales with each customer over the last twelve months, and the y-axis represents projected sales with this customer over the coming twelve months. It can also be insightful to substitute percentage growth on these two axes rather than absolute dollars. Obviously, customers with big circles in the top right quadrant are the most important and worthy of more time, energy, and resources. I have also found it illuminating to construct this chart by channel rather than by customer.

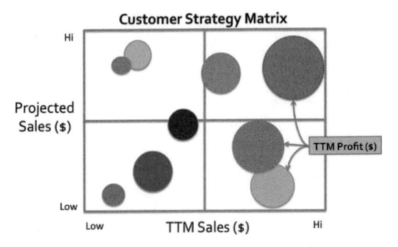

Once channels and customers have been prioritized, it's time to craft strategies for improving sales results. I have outlined on page 63 proven strategies I've learned from some of the best sales leaders in the world. Of course, your plan will depend on your industry and sales model and whether your company sells business-to-business or business-to-consumer—but selling is selling and I find these strategies largely transferable.

Sales Improvement Strategies

Goal	Strategies
Call Management	• Increase usage of inside selling, teamed with outside reps, bolstered by digital marketing tools, CRM, and ecommerce/web site. • Measure call plans completed, and elevate training and development best practices. • Coach reps to create value at most senior level of decision making.
Opportunity Management	• Coach reps on the actions required to move through the stages of the sales cycle. • Leverage new digital marketing and CRM tools. • Measure and optimize the percentage of early-stage opportunities qualified and closed. • Measure and manage stages of qualification using CRM tools. • Allocate time and energy on the opportunities that offer highest ROI using analytics.
Account Management	• Focus on working with reps to develop account plans that maximize profitable growth while dovetailing with the customers goals and strategies. • Cultivate top-to-top relationships up to CEO level to uncover strategic synergies.
Territory Management	• Rigorously allocate sales reps' time among all the customers in a given territory based on analytics. • Focus on metrics like the number of customers per rep, number of sales calls made, and even sales calls to different types of customers.

While customer intimacy is vital for all leaders, it is the end user or consumer of your products and/or services who matters most. The best leaders realize that everything must begin with their consumers, and they know that the ultimate competitive advantage is understanding and delighting them better than anyone else in the marketplace. This fact-based knowledge gives them leverage with their customers because their customers want to appeal to these consumers too. But more importantly, a deeper understanding of consumer pain-points, wants, and needs provides the springboard for ongoing product and service innovations supported by break-through marketing that persuades consumers that your company and brand(s) serve them best. It's the foundation for uniqueness, and uniqueness has been proven to be the ultimate predictor of marketplace success! Many companies think they understand their consumers, but the companies that dig deeper with rigorous analytics, constant immersion in their consumers' world, and an intentional brand-building process typically win a bigger share of the market. They also build stronger brands that stand the test of time.

The best brand builders know that they need a common platform and common language throughout their company, not just in the marketing or brand management departments, because the entire organization impacts their brand in some way. The brand building architecture I prefer, and will define later in this chapter, is a hybrid I've built over three decades of working with some of the best marketers in the world—from world class consumer packaged goods companies such as The Clorox Company, SC Johnson, and Pepsi to outstanding advertising agencies such as Foote Cone & Belding, Ogilvy & Mather, and BBDO. I created this simplified process by borrowing and combining best practices from former teammates. Together we helped build some of the strongest brands in the world, including Clorox, Formula 409, Pepsi, 7 Up, OFF!, Body Glove, Windex, Scrubbing Bubbles, Pledge, Drano, Kodak, and Fellowes Shredders. Collectively, these leaders inspired the approach I went on to mold and leverage to build new brands, reinvigorate tired brands, and turn around fledgling businesses in a wide range of industries. More recently, in my practice as a leadership consultant, I have used it in a wide variety of industries including greeting cards, education, beauty care, digital marketing services, heavy farming equipment, men's grooming, building construction products, odor eliminators, management consulting services, and even non-profit organizations and family offices. I do not present it as the only way to strategically build a brand—I've seen many different approaches with different terminologies that work—but the best approaches share the same strategic obsession with consumers.

A well-designed brand architecture ensures focus on strategy before execution, and forms a consistent foundation for strategic decisions. It also allows you to:

- Drive broad adoption of best practices
- Enable consistent execution across your company
- Control actions undermining your brand and reputation
- Build brand equity, which will become your most valuable asset
- Maximize the return on your marketing investment

Creating the brand-building architecture requires disciplined analytics focused squarely on the consumers of your products or services, and an honest assessment of the strengths and weaknesses of your brand and your organization. It includes a thorough assessment of the landscape in which you compete, an illuminating articulation of the consumer you serve (the *who*, also known as the target audience), a laser-precise definition of what you want your product or service to stand for in the hearts and minds of the *who* (the *what*, which encapsulates your brand positioning), and how you want the *who* to actually experience your product or service (the *how*, also known as execution).

The *what* is strategy, and the *how* is execution. Unfortunately, most companies don't invest enough time, energy, and resources in fully understanding the *who*. Their strategy lacks resonance, which leads to executions that are not recalled by consumers in a way that persuades them to take action. The executions or *how* that emanate from these strategies might be creative, but they don't strategically build sustained business results over time. Essentially, these strategies are tone-deaf. Most advertising fits this description, and is largely a waste of money that delivers a disappointing return on investment. But then, most companies don't adequately measure the return on their marketing investment anyway. Instead, they spend and hope, and this can give marketing a bad name, unfortunately.

When defining the *who*, you must avoid the temptation to

be all things to all people. This can be the kiss of death because it leads to a watered-down strategy and execution that might speak to everyone, but inspires no one.

Everything that can be associated with your brand should embody your strategy, including your culture.

When defining the *who*, I like using the simple consumer segmentation approach created by Brian Watkins at Quest Insights to really focus in on the nuances of your target audience.

Prioritizing Consumers

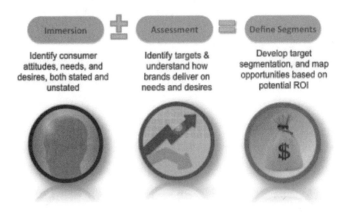

According to Watkins, defining the *what* is where the real heavy lifting happens, and it is the toughest part of creating a brand-building architecture. The *what* should detail how you want to position your product in the hearts and minds of consumers. The positioning statement defines your unique reason for being. It captures and clarifies the way you want your consumers to perceive, think, and feel about you relative to your competition. It is an articulation of why consumers should choose your brand versus competitors.

Your positioning is what you want your consumer to think about your brand, and your strategy is your attempt to build the positioning you desire.

Strategy is vital because it's the foundation for everything that touches consumers and customers, including advertising, promotions, sales materials, trade shows, SEO, paid and organic search, social media, customer service, and so on. These consumer touch points, or media vehicles, should be selected based on fact-based analysis of your consumer's media consumption behavior—not on the newest media fad. However you reach your consumers, the message should emanate from a strategy that drives consistency, integration, and synergy, making the sum of your marketing and sales efforts greater than the parts. The strategy should fuel the marketing of your brand the way a song sheet enables harmonic sounds from musicians. Ultimately, this helps you stand out and craft a unique brand.

The best strategies are fueled by an uncommon consumer understanding—a piercing insight into the target consumer's world that can serve as fertile soil for creative ideas and execution. The best consumer insights are on TRAC, an acronym shared with me by Brian Watkins and a few colleagues formerly at Procter & Gamble, one of the best marketing training grounds in the world. I embellish it a bit here with my own descriptions:

- **T**ruth—a fundamental truth about your consumer
- **R**elevant—touches upon a genuine consumer need gap, and is authentically meaningful to your brand, business, and culture
- **A**ttracts—connects strongly with your consumer and gets their attention: "Yeah, that's me!"

- Changes behavior—leads to a competitively differentiated idea that is powerful enough to persuade consumers, change behavior, and affect sales positively

When defining the *what*, it's important to focus on a key benefit, also known as a promise, that your brand offers your target audience. It should connect directly and resonate with the consumer insight. It should be the most differentiating and motivating key benefit, and you should be able to deliver it uniquely to the target audience with excellence to avoid overpromising. Key benefits should be single-minded to ensure that communications and marketing breaks through the clutter with clarity. Remember: green, red, blue, and yellow are all lovely colors when they are kept apart, but mix them together and you get brown. Focus and clarity are vital when it comes to the key benefit. There are two kinds of key benefits:

- **Functional**—a rational benefit based on performance and features. Functional benefits answer the question, "What does the product or service provide for me?"
- **Emotional**—a psychological/emotional benefit derived from the functional benefit. Emotional benefits answer the question, "How does it make me feel?"

Once you've focused on a concise and clear statement of the key benefit, it's time to detail the reasons why potential consumers should believe that your brand can deliver that key benefit you're promising. The key benefit gets consumers' attention, and the *reasons to believe* persuade consumers to take action and buy your product or service.

Remember these guidelines for homing in on the most persuasive reasons to believe:

- Show the proof that your brand can uniquely deliver the promise better than any other brand
- Make your reasons key drivers of recall and persuasion
- Make your reasons relevant to the promise, believable, and memorable
- Use visual demonstrations, genuine and compelling stories, relevant case studies, and authentic testimonials because they persuade better than mere statements

The above elements form the vital building blocks for a focused and illuminating brand-building architecture that leads to creative, memorable, and persuasive executions that ultimately fuel sales and build brand equity. The chart below illustrates the remaining elements of the brand-building architecture.

Frame of Reference:
Who your brand or product competes against

The Target:
The consumers that will find your product promise the most relevant and important

Consumer Insight:
A penetrating discovery about the motivations of your target consumer

Key Benefit:
The one functional or emotional benefit, above all others, that the brand offers

The Promise:
Your commitment to the target audience, which represents the essence of your brand

Brand Assets:
Proprietary elements that make the brand distinctive

Brand Values:
The underlying principles or ideals your brand believes in

Brand Personality:
The attributes that describe your brand as if it were a person

Reasons to Believe:
The proof of how your product delivers the key benefit

You now have a brand strategy to guide creative development of marketing and sales materials and anything else that touches consumers and customers. Now, instead of evaluating proposals based on subjective opinions and the opinions of the players in the room with the most clout, you have a fact-based road map to help guide decision-making. Of course, the only strategy the consumer sees is execution, which brings us to the *how*. The *how* is the actual articulation and delivery of the key elements of your brand/product/service to your target consumers in the most relevant and compelling way. Quite simply, it's *how* you deliver the message.

This brand-building architecture has not changed substantively in many, many years. It still works just as well today as it did fifty years ago. However, what has changed and is changing evermore rapidly are all the methods or vehicles marketers have at their disposal to reach their target consumers. Omni-channel marketing is the rage, and the explosion of digital marketing and analytical tools is opening ever-changing possibilities. But despite this, strategy still matters most. Regardless of how you reach out to your consumers, everything should emanate from this architecture to drive synergies. When marketing and sales efforts are integrated and consistent strategically, the sum is greater than the parts. When everything the consumer sees and experiences hangs together relevantly and persuasively, your efforts to build your brand and your business will achieve a more attractive ROI than if your go-to-market approach is littered with one-off and inconsistent messages, regardless of how creative they might be.

So what should leaders do to make sure their company is building a strong brand or brands? If you regularly approve or evaluate anything that your end users or consumers might see, ask to review the brand strategy or brief from which the materials were created to make sure everyone is assessing the execution from the same song sheet. From there, ask the following four simple questions to help you assess if the execution delivers the brand strategy in a way that will be memorable and persuasive to the consumer (and not necessarily to the people in the room), and is therefore worthy of your precious marketing dollars:

1. Is it on strategy?
2. Does it meet **ACT** criteria?
   - Is the idea **A**bout the key benefit or consumer promise?
   - Is the idea **C**redible?
   - Is the idea **T**hought-provoking?
3. Is it easily integrated with other executions to produce synergy?
4. Does it persuade your target to take action?

To some, my push to focus more time and energy on consumers will sound obvious, or even pedantic. But over the years I've seen many leaders lose sight of this core principle as they ascend into bigger, more demanding roles. They gradually succumb to the suction of internal forces, the temptations of instant gratification, or the escape from the daily grind offered by the executive suite. Over time, they lose sight of what is most important, and they leave this important work to others. And perhaps most concerning, they quietly send a subtle yet clear message to the troops that consumers and customers matter less.

To others this will sound idealistic because of all the demands on the leader's time. If that's you, reassess your priorities because cause and effect *will* prevail. Your consumers ultimately determine your fate. They *are* your livelihood. Understand them better than anybody, anywhere, and send a message that will exponentially enable your organization to reach a higher level of performance because your workers will want to follow your model. You set the bar, and this one should be set very high.

SUCCESS MODELS

Following graduate school, I was fortunate to land a job in brand management at The Clorox Company. It was at Clorox that I learned what it means to be truly market driven. The company's focus on consumers was relentless, rigorous, and extremely analytical. Most people think of marketing as a fairly artistic and creative craft, but at Clorox they taught us that world-class marketing demands putting consumer insights and analytics at the center of everything. Our leaders made sure everyone knew that to get ahead at Clorox you needed to deliver bottom line results, and bottom line results were best delivered by developing talented leaders and knowing your consumers better than anybody else.

This formula has served the company well since its spinoff from Procter & Gamble in 1969. What began as a bleach company quickly grew into a house of strong brands such as Formula 409, Liquid Plumr, Fresh Step, Kingsford, Hidden Valley Ranch, Pine Sol, SOS, Tilex, Brita, and Glad. Based on a solid foundation of rigorous consumer and business analytics, The Clorox Company consistently delivers new product innovations and news to the market, and they invest aggressively in memorable and persuasive marketing support to fuel profitable and sustainable growth. It's a formula that has made the company a darling of Wall Street and driven eye-popping growth in market capitalization over the last five decades.

Rust-Oleum is another company that has grown impressively by serving the market better than the competition. Their approach has been different from the one used by Clorox, showing that there are multiple ways to focus your company on the marketplace to fuel profitable growth and beat the competition. Over the last decade, Rust-Oleum has more than quintupled in size by cultivating prosperous business-building relationships with their customers, working with them to serve their consumers better than anyone else in their industry.

The best leaders realize that the day-to-day demands of running a business, or any type of organization, create powerful forces that can focus too much energy inward. They recognize their important leadership role in balancing these forces to ensure that the center of gravity of their organization is in the field with consumers and customers. As the leader, they resist the pull of the executive suite and corner office and they set the tone by being the ultimate champion of the people who purchase and use their products and services.

Chapter 5

The Lifeblood of Every Successful Business

The most successful businesses win because they do something better than anybody else. Most of them also work hard to demonstrate their superiority persuasively, and they invest in breakthrough marketing to make people aware of their solution, get them to try it, and convince them to repeatedly buy it. To remain demonstrably superior, they consistently raise the performance bar to stay ahead of their competition.

This, in essence, is how I think about innovation. It is the lifeblood of every successful business. Of course cash is king, and every successful entrepreneur will tell you that cash flow matters most. But without innovation, cash will eventually evaporate.

Servant leaders champion innovation because they understand that innovation is the lifeblood of most successful businesses that stand the test of time.

Because innovation is not a physical thing, it's hard to define. In this way, it's similar to leadership. Merriam-Webster defines innovation as a new idea, device, or method. The only thing I would add to that definition is that it must be an advancement or improvement, not just "new." Other than that, I like its definition because it suggests that innovation is not just about new products or technology. Responsibility for it should not be confined to a particular team, function, or individual within a company. It can happen in the warehouse or even the accounting department (as long as it conforms to generally accepted accounting principles and it's legal!).

While success is fueled by innovation, success can also *stifle* innovation. As a business grows and accumulates resources, leaders often put in place safety processes and practices to avoid mistakes that might undermine the success they've achieved. These practices, meant to minimize risk, can become barriers to innovation because the punishment for mistakes overwhelms the rewards for innovation, and then institutional inertia sets in. Leaders must carefully manage this delicate balance because in many companies the forces of inertia can be daunting even to the most courageous and tenacious difference-makers that the leaders depend on to raise the bar. So leaders must do much more than implore their troops to innovate in speeches and newsletters. They need to drive, fuel, and champion innovation as a way of life across their entire organization by building and nurturing a culture that embraces and unleashes it.

LEADERSHIP PRINCIPLE #5

Cultivate a performance-based culture of innovation that unleashes the innate desire in the people you lead to solve, create, and contribute to winning.

THE LEADER'S CHALLENGE

Every business needs new ideas to prosper long term. But new ideas are the natural-born enemies of the way things are. I would go so far as to say that there are more barriers to innovation than enablers in every company in the world. In many cases, the barriers are necessary. They are an integral piece of the management puzzle for buttoned-up leaders who attempt to live up to their fiduciary responsibilities with excellence. Examples include the legal function, the budgeting process, the new product development process, monthly operating reviews, and audits. They all serve vital management roles when it comes to managing risk and efficiencies. These important processes and practices help leaders avoid screwups. They were created long ago to promote discipline and align resources, increase predictability, and control behavior. These are all worthy imperatives for a business firing efficiently on all cylinders.

But when these forces are out of balance, they can also thwart the behaviors companies need to continuously raise the bar and out-innovate the competition. Big ideas, curiosity, passion, flexibility, outside-the-box thinking, and agility become the enemy. The culture evolves toward management and control more than leadership and innovation. If you're wondering where your company is on this spectrum, consider these questions:

1. Is there a common definition of innovation at your company?
2. Is innovation measured consistently across departments and divisions?
3. Are innovation success models highlighted at communications meetings for all to see?
4. Do people in your company learn from mistakes (vs. burying them)?

5. Are people in your company comfortable challenging conventional wisdom?
6. Does your incentive compensation plan reward innovation?
7. Are people in your company trained on innovation?
8. Does your entire workforce have regular access to consumer and customer insights and feedback about your products and services?
9. Does your company minimize the bureaucratic hoops that difference-makers have to jump through to get the sponsorship and resources they need to advance their business building and process improvement ideas?
10. Are front line managers held accountable and rewarded for sponsoring business-building and process-improvement initiatives?
11. Are people who solve challenging problems that stand in the way of growth acknowledged publicly for their achievement?
12. Do leaders in your organization ask "What if?" as much as they ask "Why?"
13. Does your organization fail fast on bad ideas and minimize the cost of experimentation?

If you answered "yes" more than "no" to these questions, congratulations—your culture embraces innovation. If not, your culture might need renovation.

Until now we have discussed the downside of too much control. Now let's consider the downside of too much freedom. Focusing for a moment on the new products and services aspect of innovation, let's examine what happens when a company defines innovation by the sheer number of new products and services they launch. The more, the better. In these companies, business-building ideas proliferate. They are not only sponsored by management, they are also embellished and multiplied. If a yellow widget is recommended, then management might suggest a blue widget, too. As development careens toward commercialization, teams add additional variants. The process looks like the megaphone chart below. The success or failure of these ideas is usually determined in the marketplace. And while these companies launch many new products, few achieve desired goals and survive long-term.

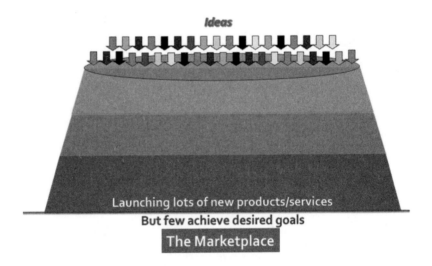

Now let's examine how it works in more disciplined, consumer-driven companies. New ideas are screened as quickly as possible using consumer-centric criteria with the intent of failing fast on bad ideas, lowering the cost of experimentation, and launching fewer, bigger, and more consumer-meaningful ideas. They use a stage-gate process to ensure broad alignment on success criteria for each gate, and they allocate precious resources to winning ideas. In these companies, the new product innovation process looks more like the funnel on page 79 than the megaphone above.

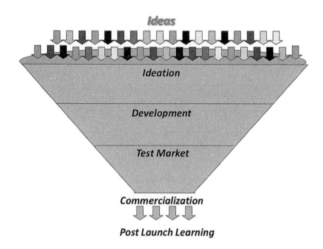

At each stage gate, cross-functional teams answer vital questions designed to predict success or failure as early as possible. Questions at the initial ideation gate include:

- Does the concept appeal to our target consumer?
- Does the idea help us achieve our vision, and is it consistent with our strategy?
- Is it feasible (for example, are we confident the idea does not violate the laws of physics)?
- Can we rapid prototype it to accelerate learning?
- Could the price-value relationship yield attractive profit margins?
- Can we do it uniquely better than anybody else, or at least faster?
- Can we supply it with service levels that meet customer expectations?
- What is the size of the prize? Could it meet our ROI hurdle?
- How can we maximize early learning while minimizing the cost of experimentation?

At the development gate, the following questions are addressed:

- Does testing of the prototype indicate we will be able to deliver the consumer promise?
- Does our marketing adequately communicate the promise and reasons to believe it?
- Can our supply chain meet quality and cost parameters?
- Have all functions met success criteria, and are they aligned?
- Does the business case clear our financial hurdles?

Before the product is launched broadly to the marketplace, teams must answer these questions:

- Does RD&E stand by the quality and integrity of the product?
- Does the final product meet consumer expectations?
- Is marketing support adequate to achieve awareness and trial goals?
- Is the supply chain prepared to meet customer expectations?
- Does the sales force have the tools they need to achieve goals?
- Do projected financials justify further investment?

Using these questions, teams can weed out bad ideas as quickly as possible and enjoy a high degree of confidence at the commercialization stage that survivors will achieve goals. The team continues to pursue learning after launch for course-correction purposes and conducts a post-mortem analysis for insight and lessons learned that can be applied to future innovation initiatives.

While this process might appear bureaucratic on the surface, in practice it can be the opposite. Each team is empowered by the freedom to avoid constant updates with management in between gates. Their contract is the success criteria at each gate (each gate has agreed upon success criteria that must be achieved to advance to the next stage of development), and they have the resources and support they need to progress to the next gate. The team seeks help from their designated sponsor/advocate whenever they need it to clear obstacles. While stage gate milestone meetings are intense and rigorous, teams operate with freedom, flexibility, and empowerment between gates.

You might look at these two different processes and ask why failing faster on bad ideas and minimizing the cost of experimentation matters so much. Let's juxtapose the two methods to highlight the benefits of the latter approach. Laying the funnel over the megaphone reveals a tremendous amount of waste in the first process.

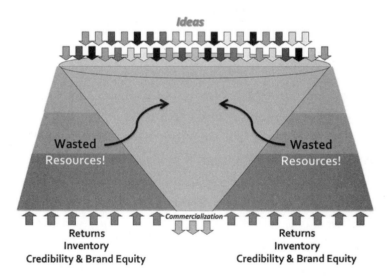

When companies rely on the broader marketplace to determine success or failure, they suffer the financial ramifications of returns, gross-to-net sales deductions from revenue, and inventory waste. They also lose brand credibility and equity as customers and consumers lose faith in their brand. And finally, all of those resources that were invested to develop and commercialize the failures could have been used to accelerate the progress of winning ideas.

I have shared two ends of the spectrum. Wherever your company lies on that spectrum, it's up to you and your leadership team to balance the forces needed to out-innovate your competition. As a leader, you have a magnifying glass in your hand with the power to focus your company's resources on the highest ROI ideas, just as you did as a youth when you harnessed the power of the sun's rays to create fire.

WHAT MATTERS MOST

I believe people take jobs and join companies with an innate desire to creatively solve problems, to make a difference, and to win. How they are greeted and treated by your culture will determine just how much of their ingenuity is accessed and leveraged as part of your workforce. The most important thing leaders can do to drive innovation is cultivate a culture that embraces and nurtures this yearning to create, solve, and contribute to winning. That might sound simple, but in most companies it requires significantly retooling management processes and practices that are often designed to do exactly the opposite.

So what does it take to create and nurture a performance-based culture of innovation and cultivate a workplace that doesn't just manage, but actually inspires passion, ingenuity, imagination and initiative—in *everyone* who touches their business, inside and outside their company walls? Here's my ten-step process to renovate your culture and maximize your chances of out-innovating the competition, based on my experience working with some of the most innovative leaders and companies in America:

1. Define and champion innovation beyond new products and services. Reveal the important role innovation plays in your company's future.
2. Train it. As a best practice, innovation is a process that is learnable. Study and steal ideas for inspiring innovation at your company from success models such as IDEO, Google, Whirlpool, and Apple.
3. Challenge everything about your business model and encourage everyone inside and outside your company to do the same. I highly recommend Gary Hamel's book, *What Matters Now*, as a foundational tool for poking at your business model with your team.
4. Spread insights that unleash the creativity and ingenuity of your people in every part of your company. Breed curiosity throughout your organization by sharing knowledge such as customer and consumer likes and dislikes, marketplace trends, technology advancements, and so forth.
5. Encourage constructive contention and diversity of thought because differences challenge assumptions, and assumptions often conceal blind spots.
6. Measure innovation consistently, everywhere. If you're not measuring it, your people quickly get the message that it's not important.
7. Reward innovation. Make it an integral component of incentive compensation and awards programs.
8. Think like an engineer, feel like an artist. Go beyond metrics and the hard stuff. Feed your culture the softer nutrients that exercise the left side of the brain.

9. Minimize unnecessary bureaucracy that stifles innovation. Challenge every single process and practice throughout your company, searching for the unintended consequences of policies, rules, and control.
10. Shift the focus of your company from managing and controlling to leading and unleashing the innate desire in all of your people to innovate.

Winning companies thrive on innovation, and innovation springs from culture. Leaders have to work hard to build and nurture a culture that shuns unnecessary bureaucracy, fails fast on bad ideas, lowers the cost of experimentation, and focuses precious resources on the highest ROI initiatives. Successful startups create this kind of culture naturally and without intention, but maintaining it over the long haul can be just as difficult as renovating an older culture at a mature company. Whatever the state of your company, it takes a lot of heavy lifting to build and sustain a performance-based culture of innovation that stands the test of time.

SUCCESS MODEL

As I sit here typing this on my amazing MacBook Air after many years of using tired personal computers, I must pick Apple as the success model for this principle, even though my only experience with the company is as a consumer and stockholder. (And one of my clients helped build their new headquarters, which is a very cool structure!)

Apple is the quintessential model when it comes to this principle. It is tempting to feature newer brands and services such as Uber, airbnb, Amazon, and Spotify because they have been so disruptive, fast, and are quickly changing consumers' lives. In fact, my daughter was recently touring Vietnam and commented on how easy it was to get around because of Uber. I laughed and said it wasn't that long ago that I almost missed a flight from New York to Chicago because I couldn't get a cab willing to take me from Manhattan to LaGuardia airport!

There are many Apple examples to choose from because Apple has created and launched so many life-changing products over the years. But my favorite innovation story is the iPod. It's easy to forget what a huge success the iPod was because Apple has done so much since. But the iPod story is most interesting to me because Sony had launched the same idea, the Walkman, many years before, and had all the technology to do it again with an innovation like the iPod. In fact, there wasn't one single shred of new technology in the iPod.

Steve Jobs delivered to consumers a user interface that blew their minds because he knew how to connect and integrate the creative forces across his company in ways that the leaders at Sony could not. While he claimed that consumer research was overvalued and consumers could not articulate what they wanted, Apple's obsession with the consumer fueled its culture of innovation and collaboration.

To give a more personal example, in 2003 the Fellowes family hired me to help them reinvigorate their family-owned company. The worldwide leader in paper shredders and the maker of the ubiquitous Banker's Box brand had stalled. While considering whether to take the role, I noticed on the Fellowes website that the company proudly proclaimed that it launched a new product *every day*. I soon learned that Fellowes was filled with many creative people but had no disciplined stage gate product development process with which to filter new product ideas.

After I came aboard, we had successes in the marketplace, but we also had many slow moving SKUs (products) and returns from customers. Inventory levels were high, and our profitability was hamstrung by too many inefficiencies.

Over the next few years we significantly improved the financial performance of the company by cleaning up the supply chain, eliminating slower selling products, and, most importantly, implementing a stage gate product development process similar to the one I've described above. We grew the business and improved profitability by focusing the creative horsepower of our people and our business partners on fewer, bigger, more market-meaningful innovations, and supporting them with improved and heightened levels of marketing support.

When people join a company, they are always excited to apply their skills, but they need leadership to help make it happen. I believe most people have an innate desire to creatively solve problems and help their organization win. The best leaders feel an extraordinary responsibility to tap into this desire to make a difference in the people they lead. They proactively cultivate a culture of innovation that embraces this yearning to create, solve, and contribute to winning. They also recognize that they must be the chief connector, as Steve Jobs called his role. These leaders go beyond rallying the troops and espousing the virtues of innovation by championing the principles, tools, and behaviors needed to unleash innovation in ways that fuel profitable and sustainable growth over the long haul.

Part Three

Fire in the Belly

(Beyond Engagement)

Chapter 6

Who's In?

You might be surprised by how many people aren't "in." That's because employees in a lot of companies operate in the dark. Their leaders mean well, but they often focus most of their attention behind closed doors with key stakeholders and senior-level teammates dealing with urgent matters. This leaves little time for open, candid communication that reaches the entire workforce with the clarity, consistency, and repetition required to fully engage people in the initiatives that are critical to the future prosperity of their company.

LEADERSHIP PRINCIPLE #6

Communicate relentlessly to give people the context they need to be "all in."

THE LEADER'S CHALLENGE

Renovating a culture requires people to change their behavior. And to change their behavior, people must be engaged and committed. Commitment requires a thorough understanding of why change is necessary, and that understanding hinges on persuasive communication from leaders at all levels of the organization.

Most leaders want the change they desire for their organization to happen like a light switch. They are action- and results-oriented. That's probably how they achieved their leadership role. They are motivated to change and they're ready to flip the switch. Unfortunately, workforce reality is more like a journey than a light switch. Many workers aren't compelled to change right away. (Of course, some people are always ready to sign up and go. They are the difference-makers that leaders must champion publicly and often, to reveal success models to their entire workforce. For more about this aspect of leadership, see chapters 1 and 9.)

The larger an organization, the more likely it is to resist new ideas. For many people, the way things are today is simply more appealing than the way they might be in a future, unknown state that their leader envisions. As I noted earlier, people don't fear change. They fear loss. Many change initiatives threaten their competence, relationships, territory, security, sense of direction, and in some cases, their livelihood. What can possibly be so important that requires embracing this kind of potential loss? To accept it, they need rational and compelling context.

The leader might think they have communicated an important message because they said it once or even a few times in key meetings and publicly to their entire organization. But it has been proven that many people need to hear a message at least *seven* times for it to sink in. That message also must persuasively answer the questions every employee will be asking: What does all this mean for me, and how can I personally help us win?

If you ask leaders how well they communicate with their workforce, most will tell you that communication is a top priority and they do it pretty well. Most leaders conduct regular communications meetings where they share goals and results, and they have other mechanisms for connecting with the people they lead. But their perception is often not reality through the eyes of their work-force. Leaders must have empathy to appreciate what their people need from them to fully commit to changing their behavior. The old command-and-control days of "You should do this because I say so" and "You should be happy to have a job" are gone. People want more. Too often, leaders deliver messages crafted through their own lens rather than through the lenses of the people they wish to inspire toward improved performance.

Recall in the introduction to this book I described why people disengage from their job and their work. Often they suffer from anonymity, irrelevance, and immeasurement. The data clearly reveals that many people in many companies are disengaged from the goals of their leaders.

Most leaders I work with initially suggest this description does not reflect their workforce. They believe that their workforce is aligned and committed to the leader's goals, their environment is open and transparent, and trust permeates their culture. My conversations with their workforce often reveal a different, sometimes brutal reality that resembles the research more than the leader's perception.

Unfortunately, even when best practices are executed at the highest levels of companies, they are often not being cascaded and implemented throughout the company with the kind of fidelity most leaders assume.

Right about now you're probably saying something like "Come on, you think this is more important than strategy or execution, or that new acquisition we're working on?" Yes, I do, because it's the engagement and commitment of your people that will ultimately determine the ROI of all of those other requisite initiatives you and your team are sweating.

You might also be thinking that your company is different, because you are different. Your people are more engaged because you lead them better than the leaders in these surveys. That might be true, but remember that your information is filtered. No matter how good you are at seeking bad news and constructive criticism, complements travel to the corner office and up the ivory tower much more smoothly than the brutal facts. The reality in many organizations is that the bulk of the workforce thinks their leaders at the top don't really care about them, and they distrust them. While your workforce might be more engaged than the average workforce, I believe all leaders should assume that this is their starting point, and work relentlessly to provide the context their workforce needs to be "all in."

WHAT MATTERS MOST

No one is obligated to follow anyone. It is increasingly an opt-in or opt-out world. Most people don't just want a job, they want to identify with a meaningful cause. They want their leaders to show authentic commitment and passion for that cause. Leaders need to help other leaders at all levels of their company paint a compelling picture of future prosperity, and they must communicate it long after they think the workforce embraces it. They must be genuine, convincing, and trustworthy champions of their enterprise's possibilities, and they must help people understand their role in helping their company win and prosper.

> **Servant leaders provide their workforce the context they need to grow and elevate their game.**

As leaders work with their team to craft their communications strategies, they should assume that their people need to progress through stages of a change journey. Leaders must persuasively communicate to a target audience that is progressing through denial, resistance, exploration, and eventually commitment. The challenge is exacerbated by the fact that there are people distributed throughout all of these stages. Knowing where your people are on the journey, and tailoring your message, is critical.

Once a leader fully appreciates the mindset of their people in these stages of the journey, she will find it easier to be receiver-based in her communications. These five communication tips for nurturing people toward full-on commitment have served me well for many years:

1. **Lead transparent "town hall" or "all-hands" meetings as the centerpiece for driving cultural transformation, engagement, and ownership.** And in these meetings, I suggest these proven methods:
   - Tie everything back to your vision, purpose, core values, strategic direction, and goals. Share progress as transparently and candidly as possible. Consistency and even repetition are critical.
   - Keep your people connected to the impact your business has on society. Don't take this connection for granted. Assume that your employees don't think about it much in their day-to-day job, and they need motivating reminders. They need you to connect them with the marketplace and external environment honestly and objectively by sharing the positive and negative facts. Give them reasons to believe in your company's purpose and promise, and be honest when you're not meeting consumer and customer expectations so they can help do something about it. Solutions can come from places you least often expect.

- Showcase difference-makers. Use these meetings to illuminate what success looks like by featuring at least one difference-maker and/or high-performing team. Let employees tell their story, and make sure they have the coaching they need to communicate their message succinctly.
- Teach your employees something important. At each meeting, include a brief session that elevates their business acumen and ability to contribute to goals. For example, include P&L 101 where you provide a simplified explanation of a profit & loss financial statement and help everyone understand his role and impact. Make these lessons relevant all the way to the factory floor and warehouse.
- Share wins and losses, and call on difference-makers in the audience to provide details.
- Illuminate your organization's core values at every meeting by shining a spotlight on employees who recently modeled the values.
- Always allow time for Q&A. If your culture is dormant, you may not hear many questions early in the journey. If you know people are concerned about something but they are unwilling to speak up, plant some really tough questions in the crowd ahead of time and answer them with candor to model the openness you seek in your culture. Be honest when you don't know the answer, and resurrect the question later when you secure an answer. Questions will grow over time as you build credibility and trust, as will transparency and alignment.

2. **Champion your company's vision, principles, strategy, and plans with external partners.** Your business partners,

customers, and suppliers want to know that your company is led by someone who understands their strategies and goals, and that you are dedicated to finding common ground upon which you can collaborate to achieve mutually beneficial results. Show them that you walk the talk of your company's purpose and promise.

3. **Maximize your time with the troops and listen to them.** Schedule "walk-around time" and treat it like an important meeting every day. Don't forget your people in more remote locations such as the field, factories, and distribution centers, as well as in international operations. It's the same way I treat physical exercise. If you don't make it a priority and schedule it, it won't happen. For example, I like doing regularly scheduled "delta breakfasts" with eight to ten employees who have diverse roles from different parts of the company. Whether you schedule a meal or coffee, have a casual discussion about your culture and the challenges your employees face in their jobs. By listening to them and showing them that you sincerely care about them, you will receive in return valuable unfiltered insight, which will give you an opportunity to reinforce your strategic direction and core values. Reinforce their role and accountability. (I borrowed this idea from Jerry Quindlen, one of the best teammates and leaders with whom I have worked. For more insight regarding connecting with and listening to the troops, Google Navy Seal Rorke Denver and watch some of his videos about being present as a leader. Good stuff.)

4. **Prioritize and participate in talent review sessions beyond your direct reports, and extend your influence deeply into the talent recruitment process.** These venues

provide an important platform for communicating servant leadership principles and the importance of talent and leadership development, and sends an important message that all supervisors in your company should care about the acquisition, development, and retention of top talent. For more on this topic, I highly recommend the article "Building a Team of A Players" by Kevin Ryan, published by the *Harvard Business Review*.

5. **Catch people doing something well.** Like coaches, many leaders either under-value or forget the impact of rewarding success and creating a model for others to emulate. Send handwritten notes and structure rewards for both exceptional results and desired behaviors. For example, I recommend giving annual President's Awards publicly at town hall meetings to employees who exhibit the company's stated core values. Make sure criteria for these awards are clearly defined and communicated. I am not suggesting that leaders should avoid tough conversations and constructive guidance when needed. But balance is key because nobody likes following a leader who is constantly playing whack-a-mole.

Communication was a vital ingredient of the recipe my leadership team and I used to turn around Recycled Paper Greetings in the face and wake of the 2008 financial crisis. We used this approach to retain our workforce despite many challenges that required us to take difficult actions, such as suspending 401k contributions and skipping merit pay increases for a year. At times we thought we might have to close the doors, but we lost no one because of the open, honest, and direct approach we utilized. Everyone kept their hands on the steering wheel and we navigated the survival and turnaround of the company together—because we communicated relentlessly.

For additional advice, I recommend the book *Unusually Excellent* by John Hamm. John understands that leaders must be able to stand in their follower's shoes and see themselves from that perspective when communicating with them. He prescribes nine leadership skills that can help leaders significantly increase the percentage of their workforce that responds affirmatively when asked, "Who's in?"

A SUCCESS MODEL

Joe Mallof joined SC Johnson Wax as president of North America in the late 1990s after a successful career at Procter & Gamble. I learned more from Joe about engaging the workforce and getting everybody on the same page than any other leader with whom I've worked.

I wasn't the only one. In fact, just one year after joining the company, the CEO at the time, Bill Perez, stated publicly at an officer's meeting that Joe had a bigger impact on SCJ in his first year than anyone he had witnessed in their first year over his three decades at the company.

Joe immediately embraced the family culture at SCJ by sitting down with everyone face to face, bringing a picture of his family, telling stories, and asking questions that showed he was genuinely interested in everyone he was leading. He also communicated relentlessly. He wasn't flashy. What you saw was what you got: a straight shooter who clearly took his leadership responsibility seriously. Joe was rarely in his office because he maximized time with the people he led and the consumers and customers we served. For example, when he approved new packaging, branding, and graphics, he did it in a store on retail shelves, not in a conference room. He worked collaboratively to get everyone aligned on a succinct, one-page strategic plan, and he taught our leadership team how to deploy it to maximize commitment. Communication was the centerpiece.

SCJ had company-wide communications meetings before Joe joined the company, but he took them to a new level by adding additional venues for genuine engagement with *all* employees. We were no longer talking at employees, but with them. Before Joe, the company repurposed one presentation for employees that prioritized the convenience of the leadership team. Under Joe's leadership, we pressed the flesh and took our message directly to all employees, regardless of location and shift. We touched everybody. Our one-time presentation morphed into a twenty-four-hour road show across several venues. Joe made sure we left no one untouched, and they responded.

As workforce commitment to achieving our shared goals improved, results followed suit. Joe leveraged SCJ's culture of innovation and family values by getting all hands on deck. More and more people knew they played a role in our collective future prosperity because Joe taught our leadership team how to engage and align an entire workforce. We were all in-it-to-win-it, together, because Joe Mallof was a leader who fully appreciated that people need context and transparent communication to sign up for and fully commit to changing behavior, culture, and ultimately bottom line results.

Chapter 7

EQ Trumps IQ

In the rough and tumble world of business, many leaders once considered softer skills such as self-awareness and empathy less important than intellectual abilities and technical skills. These hard charging leaders often questioned how effectively managers could make tough decisions if they "felt" too much for the people who might be affected. I have always believed that hard and soft skills can co-exist synergistically. I'm not suggesting that intellect and technical acumen are unimportant, but that the importance of these softer skills is frequently underestimated.

I was first exposed to the concept of emotional intelligence (EQ) while attending a leadership development program at The Center for Creative Leadership in 1994. Shortly thereafter, Daniel Goleman released his seminal book, *Emotional Intelligence,* in which he eloquently detailed the growing need for more balanced leaders who are self-aware, self-regulated, driven to succeed, empathic, and socially adept.

Early in my career, I was frequently disappointed by the lack of emotional intelligence demonstrated by many of the leaders held up as success models in the world-class companies where I toiled. I wanted to look to the executive suite and see leaders who inspired me as I worked my way up the corporate ladder. In my first job out of Purdue as a structural engineer at Bechtel, Stephen Bechtel Jr. motivated me. He was an impressive leader of a family-owned company who surrounded himself with strong leaders such as George Schulz and Casper Weinberger. But between me and them, I encountered many managers who were completely tone-deaf when it came to leading others because they were simply too consumed with their own insecurities and interests. I had worked hard in school to land a highly sought-after position at the preeminent and largest construction-engineering firm in the world, and for the most part I was disillusioned with what I encountered in the management ranks. It led me to further my education and to pursue an MBA at the University of Chicago.

A few years later as a young, emerging leader at SC Johnson, I found Goleman's ideas about EQ and their growing acceptance in the business community encouraging. In a nutshell, Goleman provided compelling evidence that emotional intelligence is twice as important as technical skills or IQ. His 1998 *Harvard Business Review* article titled "What Makes a Leader?" quickly became a classic. Goleman and his writings gave me hope that times would change—that tone-deaf executives would give way to higher EQ leaders.

Since Goleman's first book, there has been an encouraging long-term trend toward emotional enlightenment. However, remnants of the old way of thinking and behaving persist. For example, the most intellectually gifted leader for whom I ever worked turned out to be the least emotionally intelligent person I have ever known. This business owner treated people like pawns on a corporate chessboard. He knew all the right words to say, but over time he made it clear that everyone he led was an expendable asset who existed only to serve *his* needs. When times were good, he was impressive, and we could overlook his social awkwardness.

When times got tough, however, his ego and narcissism took over, and he intellectually bullied and berated people into the behaviors he desired. Most people avoided sharing bad news with him, and those courageous few who dared to speak the undesirable truth were punished, often publicly. These days, leaders like this seldom survive, but, because he owns the company, he gets away with treating people poorly. As you might expect, his company consistently underperforms because top talent eventually leaves. After the rampant turnover, this leader has been left with yes-people who avoid contention, do what they are told, and are willing to accept working in an uninspiring workplace devoid of emotion and respect. Karma ultimately prevails.

LEADERSHIP PRINCIPLE #7

Emotionally intelligent leaders cultivate healthier organizations. Great leaders model empathy and see the world through the eyes of others because EQ often trumps IQ.

THE LEADER'S CHALLENGE

It's easy to discount the softer side of leadership because the relationship of EQ to bottom line results isn't always obvious and is rarely measured. Even today there are stakeholders and board members who think you are a wimp if you even talk about this stuff! But workforce trends and values increasingly make people who ignore EQ look like dinosaurs. The continued progression of women into leadership roles is having a profound impact on the way we run companies, and the attitudes of the millennial generation are accelerating progress toward a workforce that expects more emotionally enlightened leaders. EQ matters more today than ever.

To be clear, I'm a big fan of prioritizing bottom line results and accountability. Those who don't ultimately underperform. But I also believe that the way short-term results are delivered will significantly impact an organization's ability to deliver sustainable growth. Most leaders today would agree with that statement, but how many pay serious attention to *how* the results are delivered? If it's not measured, the message received by the workforce is that it's not important. Increasingly, the workforce wants it to be important.

Servant leaders prioritize results, but they also value how results are delivered.

Most companies hold their people accountable for P&L and balance sheet metrics such as sales, costs, quality, profits, margins, inventory, cash flow, and so on. More progressive companies find ways to integrate EQ-related measurements into their assessments because EQ skills fuel collaboration, innovation, and engagement—behaviors that ultimately drive sustained profitable growth.

That is exactly what we did when I joined a family-owned education company as the new CEO to lead a turnaround after five years of declining sales. The first thing we did was define our core values and establish leadership expectations that included emotional intelligence, and then we developed a plan to turn the business around. The former was important because the culture was rife with behavior that undermined collaboration and trust. Integrity was optional, and passive-aggressive behavior was rampant. The core values, guiding principles, and clearly defined leadership expectations regarding emotional intelligence served as a critical foundation to the plan we built that ultimately transformed the culture and led to improved business results.

In many cases such as this one, the biggest challenge can be convincing stakeholders that emotional intelligence is important, and agreeing to metrics. After that it's a matter of driving execution.

I recommend building EQ metric scores into your company's performance management and rewards program because you get what you measure and reward. While about 60 to 75 percent of employee performance assessments and compensation should be based on hard metrics and results, you should hold people accountable for *how* they achieve their goals. You can do that by basing 25 to 40 percent of their assessments on their performance against clearly defined behavioral expectations that you and your leadership team agree will advance your culture toward sustained profitable growth. Your metrics should acknowledge the importance of emotional intelligence. They should also be consistent with your stated and practiced purpose and core values. I recommend a 360-degree feedback process to ensure your view of performance is holistic, not just top-down. This sends a message to the organization that these skills and behaviors matter in every interaction, just as intellectual capabilities and technical skills do. (In the next section, I'll provide more insight into the specific skills and behaviors high-EQ leaders consistently coach and develop in their companies to create a healthier culture that fuels sustainable growth.)

WHAT MATTERS MOST

Research into human psychology shows us that we tend to treat others and ourselves the way we were treated during our formative years—or else we break the cycle. Given the vast differences in ways children are treated, we all grow up with our own unique expectations of how we want to be treated. This, in part, explains why we are sometimes baffled when a friend selects a mate who we see as a serious problem. (People who were treated poorly during their formative years sometimes seek people who treat them abusively.)

The best leaders understand the vast differences of emotional needs implicitly, whether they have been taught the underlying psychology or not. These leaders invest the time and energy to get inside the heads of the people they are leading. They don't just follow the golden rule and treat people the way they personally want to be treated. They work hard to understand the formative experiences and motivations of the people they lead, and they try to see the world through the lenses of others. While they lead with unwavering principles and drive, they are agile in their dealings with others because they understand that everybody is motivated by a unique view of the world, grounded in personal, formative experiences.

This does not mean that great leaders are chameleons. Most are quite steady and consistent in their beliefs and practices. But they also have a high level of self-awareness with an acute understanding of how their feelings affect themselves, other people, and their performance. Their unwavering focus on their values and priorities makes them the enemies of politics, in-fighting, and passive-aggressive behavior. They have a clear sense of where they are headed, and most importantly, why.

Great leaders are driven to put points on the board. Not just to achieve goals, but to exceed them. In emotionally intelligent leaders, this motivation is matched by contagious optimism, even in the face of adversity. They consistently raise the performance bar, and they love keeping score and teaming with others to win. They are lifelong learners, and they seek challenges that will both stretch their capacities and strengthen their skill sets. While they take personal pride in their achievements, they also exhibit admirable commitment to their teams and the people they lead.

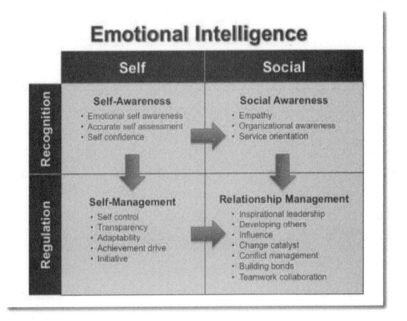

High EQ leaders foster cultures of trust and fairness and are capable of being vulnerable with the people they lead. They are in touch with their emotions and comfortable discussing feelings. This enables them to deal with ambiguity, change, and even crises with agility because they don't panic. These are the moments that set them apart. While others retreat toward self-preservation, high EQ leaders suspend judgment, analyze the situation, and draw out the best thinking in their teammates. Their extraordinary ability to self-regulate helps them make tough, principle-based decisions while appreciating the feelings of others, because they avoid confusing empathy with sympathy. This self-regulation also helps them avoid impulsive temptations, sending a powerful message to their teammates that integrity matters most in their organization. Ultimately, they bring out the best in others.

Finally, high EQ leaders work diligently to build a solid foundation of relationships with stakeholders, teammates, customers, and partners. These leaders are very good at finding common ground with a broad range of people. They are persuasive and nimble communicators, adjusting their approaches, not their principles, based on the needs of their audience and the situation. In contentious scenarios, they have the keen ability to navigate toward win-win solutions. They can see the gray when most see only black and white. They help others navigate choices that might appear to be either/or into solvable paradoxes. These leaders cultivate healthier organizations because their teammates work to emulate their collaborative and emotionally intelligent role model.

A SUCCESS MODEL

I will be forever indebted to Mary George, the chairman of the board at Recycled Paper Greetings back in 2006 when I was recruited to lead the turnaround as CEO. Mary never wavered in her support of my team—and of me personally—as we navigated extraordinary challenges such as the 2008 economic crisis, the ensuing loss of some of our most profitable customers to bankruptcy, feuding stakeholders, multiple lawsuits, and two financial restructurings.

Mary shared my burning desire to win, and she showed everyone at our company that she genuinely cared about us as human beings. We were not just pawns on the workplace chessboard. We knew that she had our backs as we fought through unprecedented headwinds and still prevailed. Mary was willing to roll up her sleeves and work with us when she could add unique value beyond the boardroom. For example, when we were struggling to gain distribution at a leading retailer due to persistent and questionable competitive roadblocks, she helped us connect higher into the retailer's organization to achieve more objective and rational consideration. She didn't just refer us to a contact and wish us well. Mary joined us on a critical sales call, and we ultimately landed the business. With her consistent support, we remained focused on our core values and strategic plan, and we were able to turn the business around and achieve most of our goals.

Mary also showed me how to cultivate game-changing relationships. She elevated my emotional intelligence to a higher level, and she taught me how to connect better with people on their terms (when my instincts were to force my own solution). Her bigger picture approach to win-win resolutions helped me become a better leader.

High EQ leaders such as Mary George breed healthier cultures that thrive on collaboration and open communication. The impact of this type of leadership is exponential. These leaders are force-multipliers, and their results are rarely one-hit wonders because talented people flock to them and are inspired to help them build upon their successes.

Chapter 8

Karma Rules

The United States of America was founded on several core principles including liberty, freedom, and equality. These specific words are repeated often in the United States Constitution. While the word *integrity* is not used pervasively in that document, the two key components of integrity—*honor* and *truth*—are. Integrity is a critical building block of what makes America exceptional. Without integrity, liberty, freedom, and equality disintegrate. The further we get from 1776, the more American citizens take for granted what our founders fought so hard for us to have. But they are not at all a given.

Servant leadership is grounded in the same kind of integrity that made America exceptional.

Many other cultures do not have these principles at the top of their priority lists. My professional life has allowed me to experience some of these cultures firsthand, and that has helped me understand this critical difference and why America is so special. For example, in some cultures, harmony is valued over integrity. But valuing harmony over integrity can open the door to destructive forces such as passive-aggressive behavior, lying, and sometimes even cheating and stealing.

I grow more and more convinced that the words I heard from my mother since early childhood are true: "What goes around, comes around." Over time I have seen good things come to those who behave with strong character and integrity. I've also witnessed the ultimate demise of people who cut corners to get ahead— those who become so obsessed with quenching the thirst of their own insecurities that they lose sight of what is right and wrong. For example, take a look at the leaders of Enron, or, more recently, at the seventy-first governor of Virginia.

I increasingly believe that the way we handle ourselves and treat others matters long term. As a leader, I can speak with great certainty to the truth that integrity has an exponential effect on the organization or team you lead.

LEADERSHIP PRINCIPLE #8

Operate transparently, deliver on your promises, and remain steadfastly focused on doing the right things. Karma eventually rules.

THE LEADER'S CHALLENGE

The farther you climb up the leadership ladder, the more challenging decisions become because the lines dividing right and wrong become much less black and white. For example, when a vital customer asks you to share the system economics of your business relationship with them, what do you do? How do you answer piercing questions about a highly confidential topic from an employee at a town hall meeting? These are just a few examples of the ongoing tests you can expect of your commitment to transparency and integrity.

In his book *How Will You Measure Your Life?*, Clayton Christensen describes how marginal thinking can tempt us into compromising our principles. He uses the concept to explain how good people, even a Rhodes Scholar such as Jeffrey Skilling, can end up in the slammer. The concept is similar to the business principle of marginal cost. People may choose to do the wrong thing because the marginal cost of doing something "just this one time" seems negligible. But the cost over time is multiplied. Christensen rightfully points out that there is a snowball effect to this kind of thinking because life is one unending stream of extenuating circumstances that tempt us to cross the line—especially as you gain more influence. One of the most striking examples of this concept resulted in the tragic demise of the British merchant bank Barings in 1995. It was precipitated by one small questionable choice by a trader that led him deeper and deeper down a treacherous path. Each step of the trader's journey appeared to be a small compromise of principle, but over time it had a compounding effect that added up to the catastrophic collapse of a 233-year-old institution.

Integrity matters even more as we grow more socially connected. Increasingly, we live our life under video surveillance. And social media has opened up our worlds. Mark Zuckerburg has suggested that people of sound character should be less fearful of social media because they have less to hide. Following this line of thinking, people who exhibit bad behavior will be more exposed in a socially connected world, and that's a good thing. It's an interesting idea. Whether you agree with him or not, social sites such as Facebook, Twitter, Instagram, Snapchat, LinkedIn, Pinterest, and so on are clearly here to stay, and they are transforming the way we communicate. Information travels at lightning speed, and consequently I do believe integrity matters more than ever.

In this increasingly connected world, leaders must assume that their most ironclad efforts to achieve confidentiality will often fail. They must be prepared for the broad scale socialization of everything. Servant leaders realize that you're either going to pro-actively and transparently manage and leverage the message, or it will eventually manage you, and you will be on your heels rather than your toes.

WHAT MATTERS MOST

My mother, whom I mentioned earlier, had a meager education. She never finished high school because her family needed her to enter the workforce early. As a single mom, she worked in the same canning factory for over four decades, and often worked supplemental jobs to make ends meet. I admired and was inspired by her work ethic. I remember her saying that she was not smart enough to lie, because one lie would lead to more lies, and she was simply not clever enough to keep track of all the lies. This always stuck with me. It's one pragmatic reason to tell the truth. But there are other reasons for those who think they *are* smart enough to keep track.

It has been my experience that people who have a good sense of personal purpose struggle less with this principle than others. They tend to be more motivated by opportunities to learn and grow, to increase their influence and responsibility, be recognized for their contributions, and help others do the same. I'm not suggesting that money is unimportant to these people because it matters to anyone who wants to put food on the table. But people who are motivated first and foremost by money without enough consideration of nobler aspirations tend to lose their moral compasses over time.

The MBA programs at top business schools teach us that our ultimate purpose as business leaders is to maximize shareholder value. While I agree with this premise and endorse the value to society that capitalism and free market competition bring, I also like Peter Drucker's assessment that "profit is not the purpose of a company, but rather a test of its validity." It's how we keep score. Money matters, as do profits. But neither money nor profits compare to the purpose of helping and building up people. Those who understand and embrace this principle usually realize that the latter priority feeds the former. Leaders can have their cake and eat it, too. Emotionally intelligent leaders with a good sense of purpose get this, and people want to follow them because they are drawn to their integrity. Conversely, leaders who don't get it are eventually discovered as egocentric, and they lose the commitment of the people they seek to lead. Karma eventually rules.

SUCCESS MODELS

I like to use an analogy or metaphor to help crystallize a point, so let's look outside the business world to the military for a success model. My favorite is documented in the New York Times best-selling book *We Were Soldiers Once . . . and Young.* It's a true story about the Vietnam war written by Lieutenant General Harold G. Moore (Ret.) and war journalist Joseph L. Galloway. The book, written in 1992, was turned into the 2002 movie *We Were Soldiers.*

Both book and movie tell how Lt. Gen. Moore recruited, developed, and led a team of four hundred soldiers into battle against four thousand Vietnamese soldiers—and won. Beneath the storyline is an insightful juxtaposition of two polar opposite approaches to leadership. Lt. Gen. Moore made a commitment to his soldiers to lead them from the front and to be the last one off the battlefield. First on, last off. The North Vietnamese Army was commanded by General Nguyen Huu An, who led his enormous force from behind, positioned in an underground control center.

Lt. Gen. Moore developed leaders and bonded with them while courageously fighting side by side. In comparison, General An treated his soldiers like expendable pawns on the chessboard of war. Because Lt. Gen Moore was on the front lines, he needed no interpretations of actions and results, so he nimbly course-corrected his team in real time around adversity to an improbable victory. Conversely, General An relied on reports from the field to make decisions in a command and control manner, away from the action. It's one of the best underdog success stories of all time, and an excellent foundation for leadership training and development.

I hesitate to use a war analogy because the challenges we face and the sacrifices we make leading businesses pale in comparison to the risks soldiers face when fighting for our freedom in war. But many of the leadership principles are transferable, especially the integrity with which Lt. General Moore selected, led, and cared for his troops. In the book and in the movie, the leaders to whom Lt. General Moore ultimately reports in Washington (analogous to stakeholders and headquarters in business) progress from being slow and out of touch with the reality of the battlefield to become vital partners who enable a successful outcome. And it wouldn't have happened without a courageous leader with integrity who fought like hell to connect headquarters with the battlefield and shift the center of gravity of the battle externally to the front lines where it belonged.

In 2004 I was having dinner with an important customer in Germany while attending a trade show when I was asked to share my favorite movies of late. I included "We Were Soldiers" in my answer. To my surprise, a woman at the end of our long table said, "That movie is about my father." After recovering from my surprise, I gathered my thoughts and asked Cecile Moore Rainey several questions. I was happy to learn that the book and movie accurately portrayed Lt. Gen Moore. Years later her brother, Steve Moore, expressed Lt. Gen Moore's valorous leadership well: "Dad always told us the first person a leader has to lead is him or herself using self-discipline coupled with the rigid ethical foundation of never lie, cheat or steal being the basis for success. We all learned to set goals, focus and move towards them without compromising our integrity." Now that's a success model worth emulating.

A couple of years later, a little more than a year after Recycled Paper Greetings (RPG) was purchased by a reputable private equity (PE) firm, was when I was hired to lead its turnaround. The two founders of RPG were wonderful men who remained partial owners and members of the board of directors. However, RPG was falling short of financial projections and was ebbing toward covenant default. The company had not achieved distribution at several large retailers as projected in the investment thesis.

As the new CEO, I worked urgently with the leadership team and board to develop a vision and strategic plan for the company's profitable growth and future prosperity. In the first six months, we successfully restructured the company and secured the financing we needed to upgrade the leadership and management capabilities. We also quickly improved same store sales by deploying a proprietary consumer testing methodology to elevate the success rate of new greeting cards, added several new artists and creative partners to boost consumer preference, streamlined the supply chain to improve quality and reduce costs, and secured new distribution at several large retailers to fuel growth.

Unfortunately, when our progress was interrupted by the economic crisis of 2008 many boutique retailers were destroyed, including some of our customers where we made the most profits. As chance would have it, we were just a few months away from securing distribution at the largest retailer in the world. Launching at this huge retailer would dwarf every task the company had undertaken in its thirty-six-year history and would require laser-like focus from our entire workforce. We knew that landing this retailer would increase our sales by over 30 percent and catapult us toward financial prosperity. To use a football analogy, we were on the one-yard line, but we were running out of the cash we needed to score fast.

We focused our team and attempted to restructure our balance sheet again, but our PE owners and second lien holders could not agree on financial terms. As we inched closer to financial insolvency, some of our first and second lien debt holders lost patience and sold some of our debt to our fiercest competitor, a much larger company. I later learned that our PE owners had previously met with this competitor to discuss a potential acquisition, and the competitor had signed a legal agreement that would preclude them from making the aggressive move they were now taking. Our PE owners filed a lawsuit, but we quickly realized that the legal system was not going to move fast enough to solve our financial challenges. The clock was ticking.

Once our competitor had purchased a significant amount of our debt, it became increasingly unclear who actually owned RPG. At a time when we were preparing for the biggest customer launch in the history of RPG, the earth beneath our feet grew progressively unstable. However, I was very fortunate to have our CFO, Ed Stassen, at my side. Ed, with rock solid integrity, did not waver throughout. Our point person at Rothschild, the firm we hired to help us manage the financial restructuring, was Neil Augustine, and he provided sage advice and guidance. As lawsuits and depositions proliferated between stakeholders and competitors, Neil helped me remain focused first and foremost on my fiduciary responsibilities as the leader of RPG. He also warned me that maintaining this focus in the face of so many distractions would not be easy. His coaching would prove invaluable because I was soon inundated with paradoxes and difficult choices.

The following months were rife with awkward and challenging moments. I found myself reporting to different constituencies who all had conflicting business objectives for the company. It became increasingly clear that what might be best for the company might not necessarily be financially best for me or my team. I kept my team steadfastly focused on the long-term financial survival of RPG, even if it meant surrendering our own financial equity in the process. I was proud that our team focused on doing the right thing with unwavering integrity.

While this job had been the most enjoyable and satisfying of my career, these nine months were also the most challenging of my life. Fortunately, I had a loving and supportive family that anchored me in what matters most, and I had the unwavering commitment of the best leadership team I had ever assembled and cultivated. We focused on running the business despite persistent meetings with law firms and restructuring advisors from all parties involved. Throughout the process, we held regular town halls with *all* of our people to transparently communicate our status. My team and I delivered the good news of marketplace progress as well as the bad news of the hard choices we had to make to survive financially while we navigated our ownership structure with stakeholders and the biggest customer launch in the history of our company. I will never forget standing in front of everyone before the Christmas holiday season and explaining that even though we were winning in the marketplace, we had to make difficult cost-cutting decisions such as suspending merit pay increases and 401K contributions.

Just a few weeks before our first ship date to our new, largest customer, I was notified that our competitor was on the verge of owning a majority of RPG. My general counsel and I met with their leadership and began negotiating the next phase of our company's journey. RPG survived as an enterprise and consumers can still buy RPG cards because we avoided financial insolvency. The company was saved, and we now reported to new owners.

Our new owners had been fierce competitors, but they treated us fairly, and we grew to be collaborative business partners. Once they achieved an insider's view of the innovations we had brought to the greeting card industry and learned *why* we had been gaining market share, my team and I were asked to stay on to lead the business forward. They then purchased the wholesale business of Papyrus and asked us to merge Papyrus and RPG. We led integration efforts into their supply chain and systems and ran the combined businesses as a stand-alone company in Chicago. Over the following eighteen months, all lawsuits were settled, and we exceeded business goals by 60 percent and integration goals by 220 percent. While my team and I were disappointed that the outcome fell short of our original goals, we were proud that we left the business healthier than it was when we started, and that consumers could find RPG and Papyrus greeting cards in more stores and online.

But I am most proud of the integrity, transparency, and courage we exhibited throughout this journey. By persistently and courageously doing what was right and standing up to adversity, we retained the trust of all vital stakeholders when many could have abandoned ship. We resiliently executed our strategy in the face of unprecedented headwinds, and we could not have done it without the commitment of everyone. We remained steadfastly focused on doing the right things, and the right things eventually came back to us.

Chapter 9

Coaching Overachievement

Leadership is about exponentially enabling the organization you lead to perform to its full potential. Many leaders have been taught that leadership requires them to be tough on the people they lead. They subscribe to the widely-held belief that they will get the most out of their colleagues by pushing them to their limits with stretch goals and a demanding style that catches faults and quickly prescribes remedies. But the best leaders know that it takes much more to optimize performance.

Servant leaders bring out the best in others.

Most of what I have to share on this topic was learned from sports coaches, not professors or business executives. As a decent multi-sport athlete during my youth and into college, I played for several outstanding coaches. They instilled in me a burning desire to win, and they taught me that together, courage, hustle, and resourcefulness make the difference between winning and losing.

Hustle often trumps talent when talent doesn't try hard enough.

My best coaches were certainly demanding, and they set a very high performance bar. But they didn't let their drive to win get in the way of motivating players to unprecedented levels of performance by consistently catching them doing something well. These coaches had a profound effect on my life, so I decided to become a coach myself and give back some of what they gave me. It's been my avocation ever since as I work to pay it forward. Over almost four decades, I've coached innumerable athletes, and I've received much more in return than I've invested. I have also learned a ton about human behavior in the process.

I have been astonished by how clueless many coaches are when it comes to motivating their players to peak performance. Many coaches spend a large percentage of their time running up and down the sidelines barking at players to fix this or that ASAP. Now I'll be the first to admit that it is rare that you can't find a player on the field or court doing something wrong, even on the most competitive and advanced teams. These coaches are determined to catch as many mistakes as possible and steer each player in the right direction, pronto.

In studying this behavior over many years, I have concluded that coaches who call out their athletes for mistakes are mostly in it for themselves. Many are former athletes who did not fully realize their sports dreams in their prime and are trying to live through the kids they now coach. While the kids might not understand the psychology behind their coach's behavior, I can often see in their eyes that their coach has lost them. Maybe not entirely, but their level of enthusiasm and desire has been stifled. Consequently,

I've coached many underdogs who have risen to conquer much more talented teams with the assistance of opposing coaches who did not know how to tap into the full potential of their players. These coaches were blinded by their own egocentric motives. They focused on controlling and fixing bad behavior, and they didn't appreciate the exponentially positive influence they could create by refocusing some of their energy on catching their players doing something well and holding them up as models for others to emulate.

Sound familiar? The parallels with business are abundant. Companies are littered with managers who elbowed and bullied their way up the ladder fueled by outsized ambition, sound technical skills, and impressive intellect, only to flame out as leaders.

LEADERSHIP PRINCIPLE #9

Servant leaders coach people to achieve more than they thought possible by revealing what success looks like, catching people doing something well, and showing their gratitude publicly. People need a model of success much more than they need a critic.

THE LEADER'S CHALLENGE

Even if you are a leader who understands this concept, you may find yourself swimming against the tide. Earlier in my career, I worked at a large company where the CEO was notoriously critical. Most meetings with him were focused on a game of "gotcha" rather than working collaboratively to build the business. He was determined to be the smartest man in the room. One wall in his office was designated the "Wall of Shame." On this wall were pictures of people who had erred, along with information documenting their blunders—the opposite of catching people doing something well. While the wall was an object of humor for some, it set a tone that mistakes would be publicly ridiculed. There was no "Wall of Fame" for good deeds.

Focusing on punishing people who exhibit unwanted behavior and poor results rather than fueling and rewarding success breeds an unhealthy culture of failure avoidance. A leader's own successful career and ascent to the top may have been driven by a keen desire to win, but disdain for bad news and failure can inadvertently send a signal that what matters most is avoiding failure. People learn to protect themselves by manipulating and editorializing information. They bend over backwards to explain why the numbers aren't really as bad as they look in an effort to avoid the "Wall of Shame." This fear of failure breeds a lack of courage and willingness to embrace smart risks that might lead to success. Rather than a vibrant culture of learning and innovation that fuels profitable growth, you'll create a cover-your-ass culture that persistently underachieves because good players can't overcome bad coaching.

This "gotcha" approach to leadership has always had its limitations, but it's increasingly ineffective in a more socially connected, transparent, and enlightened workplace that expects more from leaders.

WHAT MATTERS MOST

I realize that some will read my views on this principle and say I'm soft. However, I am not suggesting that leaders avoid critiquing performance or avoid delivering the honest feedback people need, and deserve, to improve performance. From my perspective, it's simply a matter of balance. It's not an either/or choice between being a hard-ass or a pushover. A leader can be tough, demanding, and forceful without being an egocentric jerk driven by personal insecurities.

Over the years I've read several books written by successful basketball coaches that have informed my passion for coaching overachievement. The works of John Wooden, Pat Summit, and Dean Smith are my favorites. Each of these coaches achieved monumental success by inspiring their players to achieve more than many thought possible. These three coaches positively impacted more peoples' lives than maybe any other coaches because their lessons extended well beyond their players' playing days. Each was very demanding in his or her own way, yet each consistently paused practice to put players on pedestals when they excelled. These coaches went beyond praise because they understood the value of a teachable moment. When a player elevated his game, these coaches highlighted the key ingredients others needed to emulate to perform at a higher level. Capturing and socializing that "ah-ha moment" is an exponentially powerful and force-multiplying leadership tool, and it's much more influential than criticizing someone publicly for poor performance.

While these coaches helped their team overachieve by praising desired behaviors and establishing success models for others to emulate, they were far from Pollyannas. They worked incredibly hard to ensure objectivity. They understood that leaders set the tone for their culture, and they knew how to cultivate a winner's mind-set. In *Unusually Excellent*, John Hamm insightfully details how leaders like this achieve honest and objective assessment of progress while driving their team to succeed:

> "The mind-set of winners is paradoxically aligned with the maturity of their relationship with failure. You see, they don't think that the opposite of winning is losing. *They see*

the other side of winning as not winning yet. And all the issues in between where they are now and the goal line are just clues and information they need to eventually achieve success. . . . They view the data associated with interim shortfalls and disappointments as diagnostic information that will help them correct course and improve their performance."

Leaders who coach overachievement tap into our innate human desire to make a difference. They stoke a burning desire to excel throughout their organization, and they convince everyone that together teamwork, courage, hustle, and resourcefulness can overcome. Give it everything you've got, and we'll find a way to win! No excuses.

These leaders are also self-aware enough to know that a keen desire to win can be perceived by others as intolerance of bad news and failure. They proactively attack filters that have been erected to protect them from the brutal facts by establishing measures to ensure objective assessment of performance. They send an important message when they salute and reward those who have the courage, integrity, and initiative to deliver bad news with a plan for astute and swift course correction. This encourages people to seek opportunities to improve performance rather than hide screw-ups, and it sends a message to the troops that "We are in it together." The ultimate result is a vibrant culture of collaboration and innovation that fuels sustained growth, rather than a culture that misses learning opportunities because it hides mistakes to avoid punishment.

SUCCESS MODELS

Pete Carroll has achieved the highest level of success as a college and professional football coach by lifting his players well beyond the performance many thought possible. For example, as the coach of the Seattle Seahawks, he drafted a short quarterback many experts passed on because they thought the player did not have the physical skills to succeed. Carroll saw something in Russell Wilson's character and spirit that he thought was special. He drafted him out of the University of Wisconsin in the fourth round of the NFL draft and coached him to a Super Bowl championship in just his second year in the league; an unprecedented achievement for a late-round draft choice. Carroll consistently takes players well beyond the capacities others predicted possible. His teams play with intensity and fire-in-the-belly, and he stokes the flames with a coaching style that inspires overachievement. Watch him on the sidelines, and you will see a coach persistently building players up rather than tearing them down.

For readers less interested in sports analogies, I offer another success model. James Levine is America's greatest living conductor. The seventy-three-year-old maestro directed and defined New York's incomparable Metropolitan Opera for roughly 40 years. He guided and inspired three generations of the world's best singers and became America's most influential conductor since Leonard Bernstein. Under his baton, the Met became the house of Levine.

Levine's students wax poetically about his ability to lift their performance to previously unthinkable heights by connecting with them in ways no other conductor could. For perspective, here's an excerpt from an interview with Bob Simon of National Public Radio:

Bob Simon: He [Levine] has been working with the great American mezzo soprano Stephanie Blythe since she was a student of his twenty years ago.

Stephanie Blythe: The man understands singers. He understands the psychology of singing. Which is not easy.

Bob Simon: What is the psychology of singing?

Stephanie Blythe: Well, everyone's different. You know, we're like a load of snowflakes up there. When you're up on the stage, there's an enormous amount of fear that goes along with that. You can't take a risk unless you're brave. And you can't be brave if you're looking down in the pit and you see the top of someone's head.

Bob Simon: And he gives you confidence?

Stephanie Blythe: He gives you an enormous confidence.

Fast forward to a telling discussion between Simon and Levine:

James Levine: I try to make a rehearsal room a very safe environment for a singer so that we can make improvements.

Bob Simon: When's the last time you screamed at a singer?

James Levine: Screamed?

Bob Simon: Uh-huh (affirming).

James Levine: Oh, I don't . . .

Bob Simon: . . . get really mad.

James Levine: I don't scream at people. Do you like it if people scream at you?

Bob Simon: No, not at all. But people do.

James Levine: Well I don't scream at people and people don't scream at me.

But they do play music and sing for him like they have for no one else. To me, this sounds like a wonderful success model for coaching people to higher levels of performance than anyone thought possible.

In the world of business, I have watched Patrick O'Brien leverage this principle to elevate the performance of his teammates and followers time and again. As I write this, Patrick is the CEO of Paris Presents, a cosmetics company he has led to impressive growth and financial success. Earlier in our careers, when I was leading the home cleaning division at SC Johnson, Patrick took on the stretch assignment of leading SCJ's sales force. He immediately raised the bar of expectations, charted a motivating path to success for his team, and inspired many of our sales reps to heightened levels of performance by catching people doing something well, providing candid and constructive feedback when improvement was needed, sharing success models, and rewarding difference-makers. As a peer, I valued Patrick's collaborative and collegial approach because he helped me to be a better leader too. Even though we have moved on in our careers, I still treasure getting together regularly with Patrick to share lunch or a beverage because I know that I can count on him to help me elevate my game. He is a builder of people.

I saved this ninth leadership principle for last because it is the great enabler of the previous eight principles. It puts topspin on all of them. It can fuel fire in the belly and convince followers that they are capable of raising the bar and elevating their performance. Many of us were raised to believe that adversity and tough love yields people who rise above challenges. There is no doubt in my mind that the significant adversity I navigated during the formative years of my life provided lessons and learning that spurred my achievement. But bringing out the best in others as a servant leader is much more complex than that.

While adversity made me tougher and more resilient, my coaches and mentors made a bigger difference in my life and guided me toward overachievement. Most of them were builders of people. They lifted me up by providing models of what excellence looks like, and they instilled belief in me that I could achieve what I wanted *if* I gave everything I had. That's what great leaders do. They bring out the best in others, and they find the utmost gratification in helping others achieve more than they ever thought possible.

Epilogue

Two Calls to Action

In 2014, after over a decade of leading businesses as a CEO, I decided to launch a leadership consulting firm to help other leaders achieve sustainable growth. This was not an easy decision because I valued the purpose and influence that came with the CEO roles I had earned, and I viewed the management consulting field with a high degree of skepticism based on several lukewarm experiences.

I had just landed a board of directors role at a family-owned enterprise, and was considering two offers to be a CEO again. The family firm required that I attend the weeklong Kellogg School of Management's Governing Family Enterprises program at Northwestern University. While I appreciated them funding my continued education, I was not excited about taking a week away from my schedule to do this. But I soon was very happy I had agreed to attend, as I once again found that everything happens for a reason. I was pleased to meet Professors John Ward and Ivan Lansberg along with many owners of family-owned enterprises—from the New York Times to L.L. Bean—and mid-cap and smaller businesses. To my surprise, the program was more hands-on and rigorous than I expected, and I found the experience enriching. As we navigated work sessions and report-outs, I gradually came to the realization that there are many more family-owned enterprises in the world than most people realize. In fact, roughly 65 percent of the US GDP is generated by family-owned businesses. It also began to dawn on me that many of these firms need help with strategy and leadership. After rolling up our sleeves together for a few days, a few family owners approached me seeking guidance. Over the next few days I saw that my background and experience were unique, and I had something to offer them that they could not find in most consultants or advisors. While I had the valuable experience of working at four venerable family-owned firms, I also had been trained at world-class public companies earlier in my career. In addition, I had toiled across a wide range of functions from engineering to marketing before ascending into general management roles, and I had been a CEO three times with a good track record across a variety of industries. Finally, and perhaps most importantly, I had developed a proven strategic planning and team-building process.

By the end of the family enterprise program at Kellogg, the idea of creating a different kind of consulting firm had crystalized. Rather than simply analyze and advise, I would offer to help leaders, boards, and family owners teach their leadership teams how to *build their own* strategic plans for sustainable growth leveraging the nine principles in this book. I decided to lean heavily on my experience and the fact that I had actually done it, not just studied it, as a key point of difference. My promise or value proposition to my clients would be heightened levels of workforce engagement, collaboration, innovation, accountability, and ultimately improved business results, just as I had accomplished in my career.

I'm very happy I made this detour because I have met some wonderful people as a result. It's been enormously fulfilling to see the lasting impact our work together has had on their families, their teams, and their companies. And for me personally, the breadth of work has also fulfilled my desire to stay on the steep slope of the learning curve. I feel blessed to have found my calling.

As my practice has blossomed, I have also noticed a change happening in the way people behave, and I want to end with two calls to action based on my observations. One call is for emerging leaders, and the other is for senior leaders.

While speaking recently about leadership at The Family Firm Institute's annual meeting, I was asked about the biggest obstacle I face with my clients when trying to help them improve performance. The answer is easy. Without hesitation, I said it is this thing we call "busy."

Technology was supposed to make our lives easier, and in some ways it has. But it also has addicted us to being "on" 24/7. Even worse, it seems that many managers and leaders think that being "busy" has become a badge of honor. To make my point, take note over the coming week how most people respond to you when you greet them and ask them how they are doing. Most if not all will respond by telling you how busy they have been lately. Talk about sucking the air out of the room! The reality is that most people really don't want to hear how busy we are. In fact, it's a waste of everybody's time. We could save the time we spend talking about being busy so we will be just a little less busy.

This "busy" epidemic also gets in the way of what Steven Covey called quadrant 2 activity in his landmark book *The 7 Habits of Highly Effective People:*, things that are strategically important but not urgent. In my work I am seeing more and more leaders use being "so busy" with short term pressing demands as an excuse for not doing the more strategic heavy lifting required to advance what matters most over the long haul.

FOR EMERGING LEADERS

My advice to emerging leaders is to minimize lamenting with your boss and your colleagues about how busy you are because it calls into question your maturity and your potential to advance to the next level of leadership responsibility. Instead, dedicate yourself to helping the people you lead and your colleagues make the tough decisions required to focus on what matters most and fuel sustained and profitable growth.

When you become a manager for the first time and you begin supervising other people, your sphere of influence and your responsibilities increase. Using round numbers and over-simplifying to demonstrate my point, you might only be able to get ten things done in a day, and suddenly you have one hundred tasks from which you must choose to dedicate your time. Assuming you are successful, as you move into increasing levels of influence and responsibility, you will certainly improve your management and leadership skills so that you can do more. But not at the same pace as the possible tasks multiply. For the sake of argument, at the next level you might now be able to get twelve things done in a day, but the tasks to choose from have now multiplied to one thousand as you supervise more people and increasingly work through others. This phenomenon continues at an accelerated pace up to the role of the CEO, and now you might be able to get twenty things done in a day but you are choosing from a hundred thousand opportunities for you to make a difference.

Now, with this theory as a backdrop, let's consider what your boss thinks when you complain about being so busy. Or perhaps when someone above your boss or the CEO pops into your office just to say "hi" and check in on you because she is a true servant leader. If the first thing you talk about is how busy you are because this makes you feel like a hard working, dedicated, and important manager, you are essentially saying that you are not ready for the next level of leadership responsibility in which you are expected to bring out the best in others as a servant leader. And when company leaders get together with HR to discuss who deserves consideration for development and advancement to the next level, those managers complaining constantly about how busy they are will likely not be on the list. Results matter most, of course, but leadership posture and maturity matter too. Remember that your leaders navigated those busy waters across the bridge to growth to a higher level of busyness that is well beyond what you are moaning about. Bottom line: stop complaining about how busy you are and dedicate yourself to serving the people you lead across the bridge to growth by helping them focus on the strategic priorities that will matter most. The best leaders know how to consistently make the tough choices needed to deliver extraordinary results without whining about the demands on their time.

FOR SENIOR LEADERS

The nine principles detailed in this book will help leaders tap into their teammates' innate human desire to make a difference, which will help them flourish. Work does not have to be drudgery. Work is incredibly rewarding when we feel like we have a purpose and we can make a meaningful difference in this world.

Why do so many people save the aspiration to make a difference for their avocation or retirement and accept an unfulfilling job? You hear people say it all the time: "When I retire, I'm going to give back to society and get involved in [my favorite worthy cause]." That's great, but time's a wasting. Leaders can impact people meaningfully in their work *today*. Of course they can affect people in the workplace, but a leader's impact can extend well beyond that. As a senior leader, your influence can be exponential. You affect peoples' lives in so many ways: the way they feel on the drive home, the way they greet their families when they walk in the door, the way they interact with their community, and their attitude toward life in general. Sure they own their attitudes, but as leaders we can all have a profound influence on the society in which we live.

Servant leaders understand that they can be force-multipliers. They are builders of people, first and foremost, and they have a huge sense of responsibility toward the people they lead. They also understand that the bridge to growth is not just professional, but can be personal too. They realize that employees who are thriving ultimately deliver better results throughout their lives. Businesses, schools, communities, governments, churches, or wherever employees toil benefit through the exponential impact of servant leadership because servant leaders bring out the best in others. That's why I'm convinced that servant leadership will be the last form of leadership still standing when all is said and done.

Acknowledgments

So many people have helped me over the years to get from where I started to where I am today. I know where to start my thank yous, but knowing where to stop is a difficult task. This book would not have been possible without the patience, advice, and love of my family so I must first thank my wife Kathy and my daughters Jennifer and Megan. As my partner for over four decades, Kathy taught me more about many of the principles in this book than anyone, especially EQ. I should also thank our Labrador retrievers Copper, Marley, and Kirby for the missed walks and rubdowns you endured while I scribed away. I have been fortunate that my career has been filled with many more ups than downs, but the downs would stand out much more prominently without the love and support of my family.

I want to thank Elizabeth Beller, Susan Randol, Barbara diSioudi, and Scott Kenemore for editing everything you've read. They exhibited remarkable patience with my lack of literary skills.

I must thank all of the coaches, mentors, managers, and teachers in my life. I have been blessed to work with some of the most outstanding leaders on the planet who taught me so much about leading with courage and character and bringing out the best in others. The final product of this book is ultimately the outcome of their influence on me as a leader. Those who stand out most include Mary Stiller, Sister Mary Constance, Bill Mumford, Joe Cerqueira, Jim Gresham, Mick Neeley, Karen Stiller, Professor Robert Lee, Father Phil Bowers, Scott Meyer, John Pikel, Karl Joss,

Rich Kosiba, Phil Strom, Professor George Stigler, Doug Kellam, Glenn Savage, Bill Morrissey, Mike Reilly, Scott Langmack, Peter Kendall, Chris Sinclair, Dave May, Fisk Johnson, Joe Mallof, Bill Perez, Jerry Quindlen, Jamie Fellowes, Mary George, Mike Keiser, Bill Young, John Beeder, Dr. John L. Ward, Dr. Ivan Lansberg, and Bob Conway.

I want to acknowledge the impact of my friends and colleagues on this book because of their collaboration and support over the years. While there are too many to list here, I do want to thank a few who took the time to debate these principles with me and read my material and provide me constructive feedback for improvement. Special thanks to Patrick O'Brien, Andy Pikel, Brian Watkins, Stephani Granato, Peter Schumann, Steve Schnell, Pat Mathia, Steve Hill, Julie Jacobs, Dan O'Brien, Lee Eisenstaedt, Ed Stassen, Carla Lang, Matt Pfister, Art and LoriLee Bielski and the team at Gamma Partners, Mark Martin, Tim Bennett, Eric Lent, Camille Cleveland, Chris Bauder, Mary Nelson, Tom Hakes and the team at Construction Specialties, Clayton Bolke, Roy Applequist, Linda Salem and the team at Great Plains Manufacturing, Jay Madary and the team at JVM Realty, Mike Sawant and the team at Market Ready, Kyle Bolke, Dan Zybinski, Tracy Tunney Ward and the team at Miramar Services, Mark Pacchini, Anne Smart, Laura Pikel, Jim Morgan, and Cathy Sutherland.

Last but not least, I thank my mother, Sally Rake, for showing me what it means to work hard and stand up for what you believe. She worked in the canning factory for close to fifty years, and supplemented her income waitressing or selling Tupperware. We didn't have much, but I never felt poor, and she made sure I grew up understanding that everything valuable in life beyond love should be earned, not given by entitlement. In the absence of a husband and father, she proactively connected me with mentors who role-modeled many of the core values and guiding principles detailed in this book. From an early age, she taught me to surround myself with people who would build my character and bring out the best in me. In my life that followed I was rarely the smartest or most talented person in the room or on the team, but I was never out-worked because she taught me the value of perseverance and tenacity.

Works Consulted

1. McChesney, Chris and Huling, Jim. *The 4 Disciplines of Execution*. First Free Press, April 2012.
2. Lincioni, Patrick. *The Three Signs of a Miserable Job*, Jossey-Bass, 2007.
3. Lincioni, Patrick, *The Five Dysfunctions of a Team*. Jossey-Bass 2002.
4. Lincioni, Patrick, *The Advantage*. Jossey-Bass, 2012.
5. DePree, Max, *Leadership is an Art*. Dell Publishing, 1989.
6. Covey, Stephen, *The Seven Habits of Highly Effective People*. Free Press, 1989.
7. Collins, Jim, *Good to Great*. William Collins, 2001.
8. Hamm, John, *Unusually Excellent*, John Wiley & Sons, 2011.
9. Hamel, Gary, *What Matters Now*. Jossey-Bass, 2012
10. *Summitt, Pat, Reach for the Summit: The Definite Dozen System for Succeeding at Whatever You Do*, Crown Publishing,1999.
11. MacKenzie, Gordon, *Orbiting The Giant Hairball*. Penguin Group, 1996.
12. McCullough, David, *1776*. Simon & Schuster, 2005.
13. Goodwin, Doris Kearns, *A Team of Rivals*. Simon & Schuster 2005.
14. Deaver, Michael K., *A Different Drummer*. Harper Collins, 2001.
15. Goleman, Daniel, *Emotional Intelligence*. Random House, 1995.
16. Kim, W. Chan and Mauborgne, Renee, *Blue Ocean Strategy*, HBR Press, 2005.

17. Christensen, Clayton, *How Will You Measure Your Life?* Harper Collins, 2012.

18. Sinek, Simon, *Leaders Eat Last.* Penguin, 2014.

19. Wooden, John and Jamison, Steve, *Wooden On Leadership*, McGraw Hill, 2005.

Index